CREATE
THE CHANGE
YOU WANT TO SEE

Published by Austin Bay,
Upper Black Eddy, Pennsylvania.
All rights reserved.

Printed in the United States
© Copyright 2020–Ski Swiatkowski and Jim Donovan.

Cover Design: Jim Eagle
www.jameseagle.com
For more information on foreign distribution, call 215 794-3826.
Reach us on the Internet: www.jimdonovan.com.

CREATE
THE CHANGE
YOU WANT TO SEE

Key strategies to fuel your success

Ski Swiatkowski – Jim Donovan

CONTENTS

INTRODUCTION

Your **beliefs** become your thoughts,
Your thoughts become your words,
Your words become your decisions,
Your **decisions** become your actions,
Your actions become your habits,
Your **habits** become your values,
Your values become your destiny.
— Mahatma Gandhi

*"The difference between who you
are and who you want to be in
life is found in your beliefs, your
decisions and your habits."*
Ski Swiatkowski

You're struggling to reach a major goal in your job or business. Perhaps, you have a big, audacious goal that you're dying to achieve in your personal life, but it eludes you. Or maybe, you have an idea that would have a huge impact on the lives of many others, but it continues to only be a dream.

Regardless of the scope and magnitude of your unfulfilled desire, it will require you to make strategic changes to the way you think and the actions you take. Let me explain. There are three mental elements that allow you to achieve what you want in life, or stifle every effort you make towards your goal. They are: your beliefs, your decisions and your habits.

The purpose of this book is to help you understand how these elements affect your life, and show you how to access their power to your advantage.

Through expert presentation and real life examples, you will learn how to create amazing shifts in the way you see, think and experience other people and events. With these new insights, you'll be empowered to take action, creating the change that enables you to achieve the things you want in your life.

It's natural to have aspirations that go beyond what we're experiencing in our life right now. Throughout the history of the human race, there's always been a driving force that's enabled us to evolve from a cave-dwelling species to the highly-developed creatures we are today. The growth of the arts, the advancements in knowledge and science, discovery and exploration: these were spawned from this quest for something better.

While everyone has unrealized potential and a desire to achieve more in their life, most people will not discover their true potential or achieve their highest aspirations or desires. In fact, the vast majority will never even make the attempt. Why?

Old Hindu legend says that, at one point in time, all human beings were like gods, endowed with a special divinity. However, the humans abused their divinity. The chief god, Brahma, declared that it should be taken away from the humans and hidden where it could never be found:

Brahma call a council meeting of all the gods in order to determine where to hide their divinity. "Let us bury it deep within the earth," said one god. But Brahma replied, "No, the humans are clever. They will dig into the earth and find it." Another god said, "Let us sink it in the depths of the ocean." But Brahma said, "No, they will find a way to dive into the ocean and will find it." Then a third god said, "Let us hide it at the top of the highest mountain." Brahma replied, "No, that will not work either. They will climb every mountain until they find it and once again regain their divinity."

In frustration the gods told Brahma, "We do not know where to hide it, because it seems that there is no place on earth or in the sea that human beings will not eventually reach."

After pondering long and hard, Brahma said, "This is what we shall do. We will hide their divinity deep within their own being, for humans will never think to look for it there." They all agreed that this would be the perfect hiding place, and so it was done.

This story has become reality. Humans all over the earth have been digging, diving, climbing, and exploring; searching for something more, something better and not realizing that everything they want can come from a God-given potential already within.

Author unknown

Brahma was right. We humans are always looking outside of ourselves for the answers, as well as who to blame for lack of answers. It is the uncommon individual, the dreamers, the idealists, the mavericks, who looks inward to find solutions.

What makes this pervasive behavior strange is that through poor management of our own mind, we are the ones who bury this treasure inside ourselves.

So, what do you secretly want in life? Perhaps, your desire is centered around a new career, your finance well-being, doing more of what you love, gaining balance in your life, reducing your stress, creating relationships, helping others, you need to ask yourself one question. Why don't you have it already?

Are you afraid of failure? Are you ignorant of what's blocking your achievements? Have you become so lazy and complacent that you've found it easier to convince yourself that you're absolutely satisfied with the results you currently have in life. Or is it a combination of all three that has you shackled from top to bottom?

No matter your case, our goal is to aid you in understanding how your beliefs about yourself and your world, the decisions you make in your life and the habits you form, give you the ability to overcome the fear, ignorance and laziness. You will see that how you manage these mental elements will dictate what you think, say and do. And, these actions will ultimately determine your level of achievement or struggle in life.

WHY WE WROTE THIS BOOK

Ski Swiatkowski: This book has been developing within me for many years. It is actually part of a journey to realize my own life purpose.

As a student and football player during my high school and college days, I was taught to study hard and play hard in order to achieve the outcomes I wanted. Our coaches and teachers strived to motivate us to develop and improve our performance. But while I formed a good work ethic and really enjoyed my high school and college years (maybe a bit too much at times), I had not formed a clear vision of my future. I felt as though something was missing.

After graduating college, finding a job and beginning to build a life for my future wife and me was my only focus. I was a guy, living on the surface of life, still unaware of deeper aspects of myself. But, I began to notice a strong curiosity of people; what makes them tick, what motivates them, what makes them happy, what discourages them.

As this curiosity to understand people became stronger, so did the drive to understand myself and my personal development. As odd as it may sound, I was driven to learn more about who I was and why I was here. This was not in a narcissistic way, but from an urge to fulfill a potential that I did not yet understand.

In my late twenties, I discovered the writings and recordings of Dr. Norman Vincent Peale (1898-1993), a minister and author known for his work in popularizing the concept of the power of positive thinking and its relationship to God. This revelation launched me into the exploration of personal-development for myself and others.

"You have been given great potential. Have you found it? What are you going to do with it?" said Dr. Peale. His messages had a profound effect on me. My vision was beginning to become clear. This was a pivotal point in my life. I will forever be grateful to that wonderful man.

The more I studied personal development, the more I saw how people were unaware of their God-given greatness. They were afraid to step out of their mental and physical comfort zones. They were afraid to challenge themselves to be more, to do more, and utilize what the world was offering them. They were unaware of this potential or if they realized it, they did not know what was holding them back or how to address these challenges.

I, too, struggled with many of the challenges we will discuss in this book. But that was actually a blessing. For as I studied myself and the people around me, I became more aware of the challenges people faced. I also learned how the ego-mind cleverly attempts to protect us, to keep us safe and out of danger; physically and psychologically. It convinces us that we are doing "okay" and lulls us back into the comfortable, safe cadence of our predictable daily life. But, all of this is at the cost of finding our greatness.

Because of this, I wanted to help awaken people and show them their greatest potential and eliminate the mindset that holds them back.

In 1996, a business associate and I started a venture to bring author Dr. Wayne Dyer (1940-2015) to the Philadelphia and Allentown, PA areas. Through my immersion into personal development, I had become a huge fan of Dr. Dyer. That, however, would not be enough to prepare me for what it would take to promote a big name like him.

Planning and running those events was an amazing, emotional roller coaster experience. Not just getting to meet Dr. Dyer, but learning what it took to produce an event like this. It was new venture with all of the associated problems of a start-up business. As it turned out, the events were reasonably successful from an attendance standpoint, but financially, we ended up losing money.

One of the attendees, who reached out to me after the events, was an author named Jim Donovan. We met for breakfast to get acquainted and explore how we might help each other. In our discussion, we discovered that we shared common beliefs regarding the power of the mind and its ability to create success or failure.

Originally from Staten Island, NY, Jim was an open-minded free-spirit who had traveled a long and near fatal road to his own discovery of his potential. Having hit bottom from a life of excesses, he had the opportunity to turn his life around. Another self-admitted self-help fanatic, Jim was an avid student of personal development and success principles.

At the time we met, Jim had just released his first book, *Handbook to a Happier Life*. Since then, he has gone on to become an internationally recognized self-help author, with several bestsellers to his credit.

Because of our like-mindedness, Jim and I started a mastermind group in our area. I'm a firm believer in the mastermind concept and its ability to accelerate growth. So, I saw our alignment as a way to help us reach our goals more quickly.

While people came and went as members of our group, we continued to be friends and have been meeting each Saturday for more than 20 years.

We had frequently talked about my writing a book. The excuse I kept bringing up was that I had a full-time job which I enjoyed a great deal, and which consumed a huge part of my time. Oh, and I had other excuses too, like my travel schedule, my family commitments and my daily fitness routine, etc. The fact was I was not motivated enough to do it. That and a fear of doing something I had never done before prevented me from attempting this goal. I convinced myself that I would write the book "someday." Well, as you know, someday can be a long way into the future or it may never come.

Then, one day in late 2017, I noticed that my heart rate was feeling different. While I had previously been diagnosed with benign PVCs (Premature Ventricular Contractions) back in 2012, the doctors told me that this was a common condition among the general population and that it was not a big issue, but should be monitored.

However, at this point, it seemed that I was feeling the PVCs more frequently than in the past. Of course, the stubborn male that I am, I continually postponed getting these symptoms checked out. It wasn't until early 2018 that I visited a cardiologist. After several tests and scans, my doctor told me that the PVCs had actually decreased. However, the one of the most important artery of my heart was enlarged, a potentially life threatening condition. If it were to rupture, I could bleed out in a short period of time.

The news was difficult to process. Throughout my life, I had always prided myself on being very healthy. I was rarely sick. What a reality check. Stewing in this stupor made me think about my mortality and the reason I am here on this earth. It was as if God had said, "You have been talking for a long time about this book you intend to write and how you want to help people discover the potential with which I have blessed them. I think I need to give you a little push."

Now, He had my attention. If this was really that important to my vision of why I was placed here, I needed to stop procrastinating and take action. Then, at one of our mastermind meetings, Jim said that he was thinking about writing a book about beliefs. I said, "Why don't we work on this book together?".

So, that is exactly what we did, turning each of our mastermind meetings into book brainstorming meetings.

I'm sure this collaboration made the process more difficult for Jim, as he had written all his books solo. He was constantly explaining the many nuances of writing a book to this novice author. But gradually, we plowed through all the hurdles involved with two different writing approaches and styles to bring this book to the public.

The fact is, in my heart, this book is a victory celebration. It honors that portion of my God-given potential which has become reality. A victory over human frailties and personal shortcomings.

We want to share with you, the reader, ideas and actions which will alter your life if you will but learn to think, process and take action. We also want you to learn from our struggles and challenges, from what we've experienced on our journeys and from the experiences of others.

Now, let's talk about who this book is intended to reach.

The authors believe that everyone is born with a tremendous latent potential that, if discovered and developed, enables us to make a unique contribution to this world. We were meant to discover our purpose and to pursue it. The operative work here is "if".

Henry David Thoreau said, "The mass of men lead lives of quiet desperation." They come to this point through the gradual embezzlement of their dreams by an insider; themselves.

I think this is more accurate today than in Thoreau's time. Studies show that a majority of people are working jobs from which they derive insufficient satisfaction. They struggle in the hope of earning enough money to buy happiness within the limited time they have outside of work. It should leave one wondering how they got to this point.

As children, we dream of doing great or exciting things when we become adults, visions of becoming professional athletes, entertainers and so forth. Most youth come out of high school and college full of hope for their future. They want to succeed, even if they are uncertain of which path they should follow.

But gradually, the real world inserts itself into their life. The complexity, demands, and responsibilities our culture and society imposes on them create a pressure that forces conformity on the majority of people. And so, most settle for the safe existence of a career path that was the best opportunity at the time. Well, they have to start somewhere, right?

As marriage and children come along, the hypnotic trance of life takes center stage. They are making adequate money and have some responsibility on the job. There's even a certain amount of success in their work which enables them to justify the course they are on.

Don't misunderstand what was just stated. Earning a living and supporting one's family are very important responsibilities. But how much more joy could be added to life if they discovered where and how to utilize your God-given potential.

Instead, people kick the proverbial can down the road of life with the hope of someday going after their goal. They are either not aware of their great potential, continue to find excuses why they can't pursue it, or they have just given up on it. And, goals and expectations they do have, are generally below their real potential. With each passing year, the drive to discover that true potential becomes weaker and weaker, like the light from a flashlight whose batteries are losing their charge.

Based on years of observation and studying human motivation and behavior, we estimate that 85% of people fall in this category. And the results they get in life reflect just that. As we get deeper into this book, we'll discuss causes of this under-utilized potential.

(Here's a brief research support note: A 2014 study at the University of Scranton, showed that 81% of people making New Year's resolutions ultimately did not keep them. Since it has been estimated that 65% of the US population makes New Year's resolutions, this means 12% succeed, 53% fail and 35% don't even make the attempt. That's a total of 88% who failed or didn't try.)

Of the remaining 15% of the population in our estimate, 10% actually have a sense of their greater potential. They have a hope that they will achieve greater fulfillment in a pursuit of their dreams. Many of these people will make attempts to discover and cultivate their potential, but fear and the lack of knowledge of how to tap into it continuously stifles them. The majority of the 10% group are stuck. And similar to the first group, they may make excuses or eventually give up.

The people in the final 5% are those who have discovered their potential and are tapping into it. They've made the leap to start their journey and are turning that potential into the realization of their dreams. They stumble and fall, but get back up to try again and again. And many have already found great success.

With this book, we wish to provide all readers with an understanding of why you are not achieving what you want (or not achieving it fast enough), what's blocking you, and where to start to change.

We are hoping to awaken those in the 85% group to see their potential and give them hope again.

For those in the 10% group, we want to provide you with a different perspective that will give you the courage to take the leap.

If you are in the 5% group and have already started on the journey, we want to give ideas that can strengthen and accelerate your success.

By enlightening you about the importance and power of your Beliefs, Decisions and Habits, and arming you with practical ideas which foster different thinking, we are giving you the formula to ultimately create the change you want in your life.

Jim Donovan: For thirty years, I've studied the principles of success. It has also been my privilege to write about many aspects of this subject. If you've read any of my previous books, you know how important I consider the topic of beliefs and how much they affect everything in your life. If there's one thing that will either help or hinder your likelihood of success, it is what you believe about yourself and your ability to achieve a particular goal.

> *"Whether you think you can or you*
> *think you can't, you're right."*
> Henry Ford

At one point, I started thinking about writing a new book on the subject of beliefs. However, I wasn't sure I could introduce enough fresh content without rehashing material from the previous books.

When Ski asked me about our collaborating on a book, I became excited by the idea. Since we had been meeting and discussing these principles for so many years, we shared similar views about what is necessary for someone to achieve success, but with different perspectives.

I knew instinctively that with our combined years of study and experience, working together would result in a more powerful and comprehensive message, not to mention how great it would be for me to be working with co-author, Ski Swiatkowski. As they say, "Two heads are better than one."

In this book, we wanted to extract the *key* elements from those years of discussion and present them to you. While there are many more topics involved in designing a success-filled life, beliefs, decisions and habits are core to the journey. We will, however, also touch upon some additional success components in context as we go.

As you read, you'll learn about the latest scientific discoveries proving the power of our **beliefs** and their ability to, among other things, heal your body.

You will be asked to think about the way you make **decisions**, to challenge those processes and to practice ways of thinking differently in order to create change that will support the achievement of your goals.

We'll invite you to examine your **habits**, to see how they are impacting your life, identifying whether they are serving or impeding your ability to succeed.

We'll challenge you to take action by engaging in "Activities", which will foster the retention and use of what you are learning. This will move you closer to the realization of your goals and dreams.

SEQUORA'S STORY

One of our objectives for this book is to provide stories of people we know, who have utilized the concepts presented to create the results they wanted to see in their lives. Two of the stories are about professional athletes, Vince Papale and Brian Propp. The manner in which they overcame their challenge provides tremendous proof that these principles work.

While their celebrity status as players in the National Football League (Vince Papale) and the National Hockey League (Brian Propp) makes their stories very exciting, there are also thousands of everyday people who are quietly reshaping their lives, using principles you are about to learn in this book.

One such story is that of Sequora Johnston, a young woman from our local area. What really impressed us was the fact that the journey and transformative outcome she experienced took place before she was twenty-two years old.

As a youth soccer player, Sequora was always a little heavier than her teammates. Despite her love for soccer, she didn't enjoy running. So, because of her size and lack of enthusiasm for running, she was constantly selected as the goal keeper on every team she joined.

In the spring soccer season of her eighth-grade school year, age thirteen, she was involved in a collision during a game. The result was a serious concussion. This not only put her out of soccer, but also prevented her from going to school. She found herself sleeping as much as twenty hours per day. The lack of exercise began to take its toll. She started to slowly add pounds.

Once permitted to go back to school for her freshman year, she was excited to resume playing soccer. But, two weeks after the start of school, a second concussion forced her to leave school once again. This time, she was out for six months.

Unable to gain medical clearance to return to school, she began cyber schooling. For a socially active teenager, this was a different type of challenge. The stress mounted. And, she continued to gain weight.

Told by the doctors that she could no longer participate in contact sports, she wanted a way to stay active. This was when she discovered powerlifting. The sport became a big part of her young life. She jumped into it with a super effort, spending eight or more hours a day in the gym, where she also did her cyber school work. It was no surprise that she began to excel as a powerlifter.

In addition to school work and powerlifting, she took a full-time job as a waitress at the pizza restaurant next door to the gym. This became her routine for all four years of high school.

This rigorous schedule forced Sequora into the adult world at an early age. The silver lining of this intense regiment was the unintended development of better **habits** and a good work ethic that seem difficult for many young people to acquire. A few years later, this ability to form good habits would serve her well.

As a powerlifter on the high school team, she found great success, setting world records in three lifting categories for the fifteen and sixteen year-old group in her weight class. But this sport created a problem for her, as well. She would typically struggle to lose fifteen to twenty pounds to get down to a particular competition weight class. Then, when the competition was over, she would fall into lengthy eating binges, a problem many lifters face. For her, this would typically translate into a weight gain of thirty pounds.

Add to this the fact that she was working full-time in a pizza restaurant with constant access to food made the problem worse. She was eating all the time.

Then, another health disaster struck. This time, it was herniated discs in her lower back and a sprained ankle. Unable to participate in competitive lifting or her job, she became depressed and ran for the comfort of the refrigerator. More weight gained.

This continuous weight increase took its toll on this young girl's body. As time went on, the scale began to reveal the consequences of her eating disorder. At five foot, six inches tall, she now weighed 240 pounds.

Feeling out of control, she blamed misfortune had ruined her life. Unhappy with who she had become and without any idea of what to do, she continued to eat. We will stop here to turn our attention to the core concepts within the message of this book. Later, we will return to Sequora's story and show how she created the change she wanted to see in her life.

SETTING THE STAGE FOR CHANGE

"Our success in life will be determined by how well we control our thoughts and our actions. The key to doing this is developing self-mastery."
Ski Swiatkowski

If someone gave you information that had the potential to change your life, would you test it out?

The truth is, the vast majority will say "yes," but their actions will say "no." They may read or hear the information and consciously recognize the truth of its logic. They may even begin to dip their toes in the waters of change. But studies show that most will go right back to the "safe," comfortable routines of their life. Then, they will rationalize why they did not take action.

A big part of the problem and what stops us from ever realizing our true potential is that we were never taught the universal principles that govern our lives. The ideas related here and in books of this type, such as: beliefs, habits, decisions, goals, affirmations and visualization are not officially part of any curriculum in our schools. Sadly, it is possible to devote twelve or more years obtaining a formal education and not be exposed to the concepts that can influence your level of success in life.

We rarely, if ever, are taught to question our beliefs or how they affect the things we do or don't do in life. As we get older, the tendency is to take a passive approach to the occurrences of life, never stopping to examine how or why things happen to us. And so, we tend to operate in reaction mode. Eventually, we come to believe that we have very little control of what life gives us. Perhaps, this resignation is the greatest cause of unhappiness and a lack of success or fulfillment in our life.

As you grow on your journey, you will begin to understand how these Universal Principles work and how you can employ them to take charge of your life and change your circumstances, regardless of your starting point. We want the experience of reading this book to be different for you. We want the information to have an impact, to actually change your life. For that to happen, you need to participate in this book, not just read it.

What follows are concepts which form the foundation of the change process. As you read, there may be concepts which will require you to leave the comfort zone of your current thinking. By doing so, your mind will stretch. And, a mind once stretched will not go back to its original state. We hope this will foster your mental growth in these areas and ultimately the personal change needed to create what you want to see in your life.

To help you further internalize the information, you will be provided with exercises that relate to the content covered. To truly benefit from the information in this book, it is recommended that you make a serious effort to complete each exercise.

CLARITY OF PURPOSE
AND DIRECTION

The purpose of life is not to be happy. It is to be useful, to be honorable, to be compassionate, to have it make some difference that you have lived and lived well

Ralph Waldo Emerson

Have you ever had a trip planned to some exotic or special destination? Perhaps you'd seen pictures or videos of that place which created a great amount of anticipation that fueled your excitement. In your mind, you could see yourself there having fun, enjoying the environment and activities.

Our life is similar to a planned trip and is often referred to as a journey. When we know which course to take in our lives, we can pinpoint the destinations that stimulate growth and success. It is important that we embark on the journeys that excite us.

This is why we need a purpose. It's like a compass that points to our true north. Real clarity about our purpose will reveal our direction and lead to options for us to pursue as vocations or avocations. It will also drive us forward, giving us a sense of value as we follow it and supplying us with the strength needed when the trip gets tough, as it sometimes does.

On the other hand, if we don't know where we are going or if the direction is very vague, there is little interest or excitement. There is nothing that will captivate us with that sense of value that will stimulate our minds and emotions. For many people, their life journey is just the same trip around the same block, day after day.

So, before you can effectively explore foundational principles of creating change in your life and tapping into your greatness, you must gain clarity of your life purpose. You must have a vision of what you could and should be doing, which will bring satisfaction and joy to you, and perhaps, contribute to the world in some positive way, big or small.

Understand that we're not implying that you need to have a life purpose as monumental as finding a cure for cancer. If that's what comes out of this exploration of your purpose, awesome. But not everyone gets a calling that big. Your goal should simply be to find what will bring you that sense of fulfillment regardless of its size.

Unfortunately, most of us rarely if ever give this topic much thought. Why? Because it's difficult, intimidating and sometimes painful to think about a subject as deep as this. And, to cause this process to be even more complicated and challenging, it might require us to make major adjustments as we go through different phases of our life.

People find it much easier to just avoid the risk and related stress, play it safe and stick with what we currently have which keeps us comfortable, rarely venturing out of our comfort zone unless forced to do so.

We, the authors, belief that everyone is blessed with certain gifts that are the basis for our purpose; our greatness. It is up to each of us to identify and cultivate those gifts for they will determine the passions and careers we pursue in life.

Some of us find it very early. A great example of this is my daughter Ali Swiatkowski and her love of animals. As a youth, she was always saving injured birds or small critters. In 6th grade, while doing research for a science report on pigs, she found out how highly intelligent these animals are. This had a big emotional impact on her. At that point, she decided to become a vegetarian. Her purpose was beginning to show itself.

Today, a successful business woman, she is a passionate animal activist. This includes being a member of the board of directors and marketing director for a local non-profit organization which raises funds for non-kill animal shelters.

She has personally rescued, fostered and found loving homes for over a dozen homeless dogs. Leveraging her business skills, she has continued to pursue her purpose in significant ways, which lead to the launch of her animal rescue website - Rescue Broad (www.rescuebroad. com).

For most of us, it's probably not that easy to identify our purpose. We might find our way into a particular industry or career. After that, the flow of the river of life seems to take over, moving us in directions not necessarily of our choosing, at least not consciously.

For those of us who are not quite sure of our purpose and the goals that come from it, let's give a starting point for development. Before we begin, understand that this exercise is designed to encourage you to examine your life and come up with interests and areas for you to explore. You may even have something jump out and grab you. You'll say, "Wow! That's it!" Or, it may be a slower process as you investigate options.

The amazing thing is that whatever you come up with has actually been there for some time. Life may have been giving you subtle signs all along. You just weren't open to the possibilities, weren't aware of it, or you may have been suppressing it.

This starting point comes from the theory of multiple intelligences, which was introduced by psychologist Dr. Howard Gardner in 1983. He concluded that the traditional view of one's intelligence quotient (IQ) is limited. With these multiple intelligences, we can account for and develop greater possibilities of human potential.

According to Gardner, these intelligences are related to:

> Linguistic-Verbal Intelligence (Words)
> Logical-Mathematical intelligence (Numbers or logic)
> Spatial Intelligence (Pictures)
> Musical Intelligence (Music)
> Intrapersonal Intelligence (Self-reflection)
> Bodily-Kinesthetic Intelligence (A physical experience)
> Interpersonal Intelligence (A social experience)
> Naturalist Intelligence (An experience in the natural world)

The theory suggests that these intelligences are a combination of inherited potential within the genetic makeup of a person and skills that can be developed in various ways through related experience.

Here are brief explanations of each intelligence. Take some notes as you find information that strikes a chord within you.

LINGUISTIC-VERBAL INTELLIGENCE

Strengths and characteristics: The ability to use writing, verbal or auditory skills to communicate complicated concepts and messages. Use of words, language, writing and information retention (verbal or written). These people have an affinity for reading, writing, speaking and communication in various forms. They are able to express themselves well.

Some Potential Careers: Writer/journalist, Editor. Lawyer, Teacher, Actor, Politician, Public Speaker, Trainer, Comedian, Speech Therapist, Newscaster/ Broadcaster, Language Translator/ Interpreter.

LOGICAL-MATHEMATICAL INTELLIGENCE

Strengths and characteristics: The ability to work with numbers, reasoning and understand concepts of math, science and logic. These people can reason, recognize patterns, logically analyze problems, can think conceptually and solving complex computations.

Potential Careers Include: Engineer, CPA/Accountant, Auditor, Scientist, Mathematician, Computer Programmer, Physician, Statistician, Pharmacist, Financial Analyst, Financial Manager.

VISUAL-SPATIAL INTELLIGENCE

Strengths and characteristics: These people have good visual and spatial judgment. That is, they visualize things easily. They can often think and see things in multiple dimensions and are good conveying images and visual representation. The ability to work with charts, videos, pictures and other visual mediums. They may enjoy painting, drawing, sculpting and other visual arts.

Potential Careers Include: Engineer, Architect, Artist, Graphic Design/ Artist, Photographer, Fashion Designer, Interior Designer, Computer Programmer, Space Design/ Planner

MUSICAL INTELLIGENCE

Strengths and characteristics: These people have strong musical intelligence and understanding of musical structure, pitch, melody and tone. They are able to think in patterns, rhythms, and sounds. They are likely to composition and performance musical creations of their own and others. Playing musical instruments and singing typically comes easy to them.

Potential Careers Include: Musician, Composer, Singer, Music teacher, Conductor, Dancer, Promoter, Songwriter, Choir Director, Music Teacher, Music Therapist, Vocal Coach/ Teacher.

INTRAPERSONAL INTELLIGENCE

Strengths and characteristics: These individuals are introspective and self-reflective with an awareness of their own motivations, feelings and emotions. They can analyze their own strengths and weaknesses as well as the basis for their own feelings and those of others.

Potential Careers Include: Writer, Philosopher, Therapist, Social Scientist, Actor, Consultant, Psychologist, Coach, Theologian, Entrepreneur/ Small Business Owner, and Counselor (Spiritual, Personal, Career or Wellness)

BODILY-KINESTHETIC INTELLIGENCE

Strengths and characteristics: Proficiency with physical movement and motor control. This means they are good at body movement, performing physical actions including hand-eye coordination, manual dexterity/ creation and body control. They combine the body and the mind through doing, versus seeing or hearing.

Potential Careers Include: Athlete, Dancer, Actor, Builder/ Carpenter, Firefighter, Law Enforcement, Physical Therapist/ Personal Trainer, Farmer, Plumber, Electrician, Sculptor, Mechanic

INTERPERSONAL INTELLIGENCE

Strengths and characteristics: These individuals have the ability to understand and relate to other people because of their ability to see and think from different perspectives. They work well through verbal and non-verbal skills to assess the desires, emotions, motivations, and intentions of people they interact with.

Potential Careers Include: Salesperson, Manager, Nurse, Mediator, Teacher, Psychologist, Philosopher, Counselor, Politician, Customer Service Representative, Receptionist, Social Worker, Coach

NATURALISTIC INTELLIGENCE

Strengths and characteristics: These people tend to have connection/ relationships to nature. They are a nurturing personality who is interested in aspects of our physical world and how it is changing. Outdoor activities are their enjoyment (hiking, canoeing, camping, gardening, etc). Love to learn things associated to nature (animals, plants and the environment).

Potential Careers Include: Animal Trainer, Veterinarian, Vet Technician, Biologist, Conservationist, Ecologist, Gardener, Forest Ranger, Farmer, Landscaper, Marine Biologist, Zookeeper, Environmentalist, Wilderness Guide.

Gardner developed this theory in an effort to improve the way people were educated by having their propensities be the guide. The reason of introducing this theory of multiple intelligence here is to help you understand and see your own inclinations, strengths and preferences which you can leverage in discovering your purpose you work through the purpose discovery exercise.

So, what intelligences resonated with you? Had you made any notes? Personally, I have a strong association with the Linguistic-Verbal, Intrapersonal and Interpersonal Intelligences described above.

(A note about the following exercise and the other action steps in this book: Most readers will skip over them. Don't be that person. Take control of your life by doing the action steps. If you are sincere about creating the change you want to see in your life, just do it.

▌ ACTIVITY STEP

On a sheet of paper or a Word document on your computer, type the heading, "My Purpose Discovery Worksheet."

Beneath the title, record any of the Intelligences listed above with which you associate and any of those strengths or characteristics you feel relate to you.

Do a brainstorming session with yourself to create two lists (brainstorming meaning: catalog free-flowing ideas without filtering or judging the immediate thought).

The first is a list of any area that you love, have found to be fascinating, interesting, enjoyable or important to you.

Look back in your life from your childhood to present day and think about what interests you've had. Did they evolve once you became a teenager? What are your interests now? To be comprehensive, you should be both broad and specific. Meaning that if your interests lie with nature as whole, that would be considered broad since there are so many aspects to nature. However, if your interest within nature is gardening, that would be considered specific. Don't be judgmental. Just write what flows to your mind. Come up with a list of at least 20 things. Next prioritize the list according to which stirs the most interest for you

The second list is your skills and talents. These should be things you are good at doing, that come easy to you or are natural areas of strength.

Review your past as you did for the first list. Be sure to record both hard skills (you are a talented painter or computer programmer) and soft skills (you are a very good listener, have great time management ability or work well under pressure). Keep in mind that you do not have to have a PhD in a particular area to place it on this list. The idea is to give you a sense of how much you actually have going for yourself and to provide you with areas to begin to explore in greater depth. Create a list of at least 10. Then put them into priority order.

For each of the top 4 items from each list, write down any feelings, qualities, values and actions that you associate with these areas or that you experienced when you engaged in them.

From these feelings, qualities, values and actions, draft a statement that expresses how they motivate or inspire you in a particular direction. (see sample below)

This is a first draft of your purpose statement. It's a process that may require multiple versions to settle on one you like. Show it to those who know you best to get some validation that you are on the right path.

For example, here are the top 4 from each of my lists: Personal Development, Performance Improvement, Leadership, Public Speaking, Teaching, Coaching, Business Development and Strategic Planning.

Then, after studying them and the feelings, qualities, values and actions they triggered, I craft this purpose statement:

> *"My purpose is to impact people's lives by using my interpersonal and communication skills to help them discover their God-given potential and to develop it, in order that they may increase their value and contribution to the world."*

Sounds a bit like a teacher or a coach, doesn't it? I believe that long before I defined my purpose, the essence of this thought is what drew me to coaching high school lacrosse as well as training business people for roughly 30 years.

These are my passions. Do you see the connection? Your purpose will compel you to find passions that enable you to express that purpose. My passions have change over the years, but my purpose has remained close to the one you see above.

> *Your feelings and emotions are your strongest indicator if your life is moving in a purposeful direction or not, so listen closely to how you feel* - Rebecca Rosen

To help prime your mind for this process, here are a few *Purpose Statements* contributed by others:

> *"To serve others in a way that magnifies my gifts and talents, while enjoying the outdoors and being an amazing wife, mother and friend."*
>
> *"To touch every single person I meet and make a huge difference in every area of their lives in an exciting, fun way."*
>
> *"I want to utilize my talents in writing and communication to grow relationships and to encourage and improve others around me."*
>
> *"To beat depression in order to live an independent, fruitful life and to help others like me to do the same."*
>
> *"I want to live up to my potential in all areas of my life and to embrace all the adventures life offers to me and in the process, help others achieve their dreams."*
>
> *"My objective in life is to impact everyone I interact with in a lasting way through music and the arts.*
>
> *"To use health and fitness to develop my mind and body so I can be an example of discipline and hard work to my family and friends, to inspire them to take care of themselves as well."*

Congratulations, you've completed your Purpose Statement. This is the foundation on which you build a life of real value. This is your BIG "WHY". There will be other "why's" that will motivate you, but this is your BIG WHY.

Remember, there is no right or wrong with this exercise. It is an expression of what you feel and the creation of a starting point that you can continue to craft.

PASSION ACTIVITY

Now, that you have at least a draft of your purpose statement, let's go a little deeper to discover your passion(s). There are potentially many ways in which you can realize your purpose. So, your goal should be to find the area or areas that provide the most pleasure and value.

For some people, your job or business will be a passion area and if it is, that would be a huge bonus. But that won't be the case for many others.

It could be something that starts as an avocation and develops into a career. Or it may be that your job is the vehicle that enables you to follow a passion that really satisfies your purpose. Here again, you need to stay open to your instincts.

Go back to your first 2 lists you created and the list of Intelligences. Review these with your newly created purpose statement in mind. This should give you some potential directions for your passion. Look for where and how your purpose can be most fulfilled. Also, be open to how your purpose can manifest in your ideal vocation and/or avocation.

Here are some questions and thoughts to further stimulate your thinking. Once again, do not filter your ideas. Just write them down.

If money were not an issue, what would you do?

What makes you feel authentic?

What activities cause you to lose track of time?

What are you doing when you are most productive? Why?

If you knew you wouldn't fail, what would you do?

If you could design you own job, how would you describe it?

Describe the ideal work day.

What is something you continually tell yourself you'll do "someday"?

When you are finished, you should have one or more passion areas identified.

Set a goal to increase involvement or investigate one new area.

Realize that this process is a continuing journey, not a single destination.

The journey might take you to a variety of passions. Be sure to enjoy the trip.

WHAT IS SUCCESS?

So, you now have an idea of your purpose, your big "why," and hopefully some specific areas that will enable you to live that purpose. It may not be a big career change (but for some, it might). It could be subtle shifts in what you are currently doing.

Before we delve into the key elements that create the change that will fuel our success, it is appropriate to define what success actually is.

If you ask 50 people the definition of success, you'll likely get 50 different answers, mainly associated with subjects such as money, prestige, power, material wealth, etc.

It's unfortunate. They should be viewed as byproducts of success, not success itself.

Perhaps it is in Earl Nightingale's seminal recording, "The Strangest Secret," that we find the best definition of success. He says, "Success is the progressive realization of a worthy ideal." But what does that mean?

Let's look at the second part of that quote first. Think of that "worthy ideal" as a dream or thought about something you want to be, do or have. Not just any thought or dream, but one that triggers a special feeling inside you, one that inspires excellence and a positive outcome. This is a starting point for success.

An ideal is defined as an ultimate object or aim of endeavor, especially one of high or noble character. A "worthy" ideal would be something that provides value or an impact on your life or the lives of others.

It's easy enough to think this worthy ideal has to be something big like pursuing a career change, advancing your education, starting a business or writing a book. But a worthy ideal could also be wanting to coach a youth sports team, or volunteering to teach struggling students to read at the local elementary school or helping at an animal rescue. As you can see, a worthy ideal is broad enough to potentially encompass many aspects of our lives. And by the way, we often don't realize that many of those seemingly small ideals can have a big impact somewhere down the road, especially on others.

The first part of the definition is just as vital to the definition of success. "The progressive realization" implies continuous momentum-building action in the direction of that "worthy ideal." You see, without action, your "worthy ideal" will merely remain a dream. As you have probably noticed in your own life that while dreams are wonderful to have, they are a dime a dozen. In other words, talk is cheap. It is taking action that transforms dreams into reality.

And note that it is not stated as, the "completion" of a worthy ideal, referring to an end result, but is the "progressive" realization of a worthy ideal. Said differently, it is the gradual striving to achieve a worthy ideal that makes one successful, not just the arrival at a specific outcome. It is also about who we become through the process that defines someone as successful.

It's interesting to note, when you combine the two parts of Earl Nightingale's definition, the worthy ideal and the progressive realization, and look around in the world (and your own life), you can see many examples that go beyond money, power, wealth and prestige as defining success.

SUCCESS IS A PROCESS

While we are on the subject of success, there's a critical aspect of this topic that needs to be addressed. Failure. While many people view failure as the opposite of success, we view it as a stepping stone to success, or a part of the success process.

It is extremely rare when you hear or read about someone who has not experienced some form of failure in the success process. More often than not, they will run into some hard lessons, as they should. Failure is a huge component to growth. It makes us smarter and more resilient in our pursuit of "worthy ideal."

Don't think of failure as negative. Embrace it. Failure can make you stronger and prepare you for your ultimate success.

This may sound strange, but the discussion of failure being part of success brings to mind Nick Foles, the former back-up quarterback of the Philadelphia Eagles and MVP of Super Bowl LII.

His career rollercoaster ride went from being selected to the Pro Bowl as an Eagle in 2013 and being named that game's offensive MVP, to being traded to the Rams in 2015, to being benched by the Rams in his first season there and then released by them in 2016.

At that point, Nick was questioning himself and his ability. He thought about quitting his professional career as a football player. After much prayer and soul-searching, he decided to sign as a back-up quarterback with the Kansas City Chiefs and his former coach, Andy Reid. It looked as if his career was showing signs of life.

But that only lasted one year as the Chiefs would not pick up the second option year on his contract. It was at that point that his original team, the Philadelphia Eagles, offered him a two-year contract to back-up their young franchise starting quarterback, Carson Wentz.

As a back-up, with little opportunity to play, he watched from the sidelines as his new friend, Carson Wentz, led the Eagles to a 10-2 record through the first twelve games in 2017. During the thirteenth game, Carson went down with a season ending knee injury. Suddenly, Nick was thrust into the starting position.

Through the final 3 regular season games heading into the playoffs, Nick showed flashes of greatness and struggle. Most of the fans and the media questioned his ability to successfully lead the talented Eagles into and through the NFL playoffs.

Although underdogs in every game, Nick and his Eagle teammates went on to defeat the previous year's NFC champion, Atlanta Falcons, and the league dominant

Minnesota Vikings to win the NFC championship and the right to face Tom Brady (arguably the greatest quarter-back of all time), genius head coach, Bill Belichick and the ultra-talented New England Patriots in the Super Bowl.

In Super Bowl LII, the Eagles out-dueled the Patriots in a game that set a record for the most yards of total offense in any NFL game ever played. And the MVP of the game was Nick Foles.

In his book, "Believe It", he credits his failure and faith in God for his success.

As in any journey, you need to prepare yourself as much as possible for what lays ahead. That's what this book is intended to do; help you prepare for the challenges and adventures that will be part of your life by giving you the tools for creating success.

Realize that each of us are born with God-given *potential*. For potential is like a vein of gold buried under the earth which must be discovered and extracted before it has any value. In the previous material covered, we tried to help you discover where that vein of gold is. Next, we'll try to help you to develop it.

RAISING YOUR SELF-AWARENESS

"Awareness is not a school quiz
that can be passed by reading
and memorizing some facts. It's a
journey that is fueled by our intent
to be open, honest, and free."
Joseph Deitch, Elevate:
An Essential Guide to Life

In the 1999 sci-fi movie, *The Matrix,* the minds of humans are forced to live in a dream world created by a computer program that simulates reality while their bodies are actually resting in human farms. At these farms, the body's energy is extracted for use by the super intelligent machines that hold them captive. The humans were not conscious of their true realty.

The movie depicts a small group of rebels who want to liberate humanity from this illusionary world by awakening people to the reality of their captivity.

While the personal plot of our lives is not as nefarious as the movie, there is a curious similarity between the way that our lives operate and the storyline of the movie. The similarity is this, instead of humans living in an unconscious state created by machines, we live in a frequently unconscious state created by our own mind, driven by the ego.

As people move through their day, they operate in varying states between consciousness and unconsciousness. A large portion of our functions and activities are done unconsciously. They are run by subconscious programs in our mind, which create shortcuts to make life easier and less difficult to navigate. But as we'll discover, there are times when our reliance on these programs create problems.

Let's give a simple example. How much thought do you give to the activities you perform from the time your alarm goes off in the morning on a workday to the time you arrive at work? Unless a disruption occurs somewhere along the way or you have a scheduled deviation in the routine, the odds are most everything you do is an automatic ritual.

You may have a routine that goes like this. You get out of bed on the same side each day. Jump into the shower.

Get dressed (briefly stopping to choose what you'll wear). Eat breakfast (maybe even the same thing most days). Brush your teeth. Get into your car. Drive to work using the same route you take every day.

How much conscious thought was used? Most everything you did required little or no thought. You were running on a series of little programs.

Here is another demonstration: What do you typically say when a casual acquaintance asks "how are you?" Odds are you have a standard response. You might say, "Good" or "I'm good", or "I'm doing okay". Now, in actuality, you may have some major problems going, but a program kicks in when that casual acquaintance acknowledges you, which triggers a mindless response.

The point is, most of the time, you don't stop to evaluate "how am I doing?" or "how shall I answer" before responding. Your internal program just plays the response through your vocal cords and mouth. This is what society refers to as autopilot.

For you to be able to create change in your life, you must start to be more conscious, more aware of your thoughts and actions as you go through your day. This is especially true regarding your interactions with other.

Regarding awareness, your goal should be to become a keen observer of your life. The ability to look and study the experiences and interactions that occur, without making ego-driven judgements or reactions, is integral to personal growth.

One way to help become the observer is to think of your life as a game. We'll use Monopoly for our example. As the player, you are represented by one of the small player pieces like the top hat, the racing car or the Scottie dog. You roll the dice and move the piece around the board of life, occasionally winning some money or acquiring a property. Those are the fun parts of the game.

Unfortunately, there are those times you land on a property owned by someone else. They have several hotels on their property square, which means you pay them a large amount of game money as rent. Or, you land on a square that requires you to draw a "Chance Card" and it says that you must go directly to jail and miss opportunities to advance your game piece.

Here's why this is a great metaphor for life and our need to become more aware. Most people unconsciously allow themselves to become like those game pieces. They are no longer the person playing the game of life at a conscious level, but a pawn that is subject to every single roll of the dice. They become embroiled in all of the twists and turns, ups and downs that life throws at them, trying to deal with the positive and negative impacts. Being the game piece becomes quite stressful and it is difficult to have any objectivity in that position.

Now, imagine that you push yourself up and away from the surface of the game board. You are no longer the player piece, but the player, the person sitting and looking down on the game board of life. That is, you become the observer of the game.

Think of each experience or interaction during your day as a roll of the dice. From the position of the observer, you have the ability to be more objective about what is happening. Can you see how you are better able to play the game more effectively with the perspective of the player versus the perspective of the piece down on the game board? This is the conscious awareness.

When people take the time to learn how to become more aware of what is happening in their life and are honest with themselves, it becomes much easier to see the gap between their current circumstances and the tremendous possibilities for their future.

It may seem obvious that everyone knows they have additional potential or that they could improve in the roles they play in life. But the truth is, most only know it at an academic level.

At a practical level, the question is, do they really believe they can achieve their potential and do they actually know how to make it materialize? And if they do, why aren't they tapping into that potential or why are they struggling to improve in those areas that they say are important?

These are the types of questions that flow from a state of awareness. As you practice becoming more aware and raising your level of consciousness, things will slow down enough for you to be able to regularly ask questions like these. This will then aid you in seeing your greater potential and producing ideas for accessing it.

THINK DIFFERENTLY - CHALLENGE YOUR CURRENT WAYS OF THINKING

*"Be open to everything and
attached to nothing."*
Wayne Dyer

As you have seen, if you want to manifest change in the substance of your life, it means manifesting change in yourself first. Personal development starts with altering your thought processes. In order to change the way you think, you must be able to open your mind to new, different and often uncomfortable possibilities.

Before we go any further, let's define a few terms we will using through this book. We'll keep them simple.

Thinking is the conscious or unconscious process of using one's mind to consider or reason about something.

Consciousness is the state or level of awareness relative to external objects or something within yourself.

Ego is a complex construct of the mind which is present at the conscious and the unconscious level. It provides a sense of personal identity (self-image) that separates itself from the rest of the world.

Imagine the ego as a ball of string that has been created through the gradual accumulation of millions of various small bits of string that represent the past experiences, feelings, and thoughts of our life. It defines, in our minds, who we are. And, to a great extent, it takes on the role to defend that sense of self.

Learning to think differently is not easy. That is because we become complacent about our usual thought routine. The act of making any change to this vital capacity requires great awareness and effort. Since we review this change as difficult, we avoid or resist it by clinging to and protect our old thought processes. It is this close-mindedness that shuts us off from opportunities to expand our views of our world and mental growth.

Additionally, we tend to like things and people that agree with or conform to our beliefs and opinions. This behavior is largely controlled by your ego; which always wants to be right. To facilitate its control, your ego directs the brain to seek information that supports those beliefs and opinions.

Think of open-mindedness as a continuum. At one extreme is total open-mindedness with total closed mindedness at the other end and varying levels in between. Every individual will hold different positions along the continuum depending on the issue being evaluated. However, generally speaking, because of the influence of their ego, the majority of people will do most of their evaluation and thinking from the closed-minded half of the continuum, using their open-mindedness when it is convenient and not threatening to their beliefs and opinions. The stronger the belief or opinion, the more this will be true.

Of course, most of us think that we are open-minded. We tend to scan our memories for situations where we demonstrated an open-mindedness in order to confirm that thinking. And therein lies the danger. We have a blind spot to our closed-mindedness until we make a conscious effort to entertain opposing viewpoints without judging them. That means controlling the ego during our thought process, suspending judgement and permitting the possibility that beliefs and opinions could be wrong. This may be difficult to do, especially if you hold a strong opposing belief. In essence, you are purposefully creating a conflict or cognitive dissonance for you to consider.

Proactive thinking is tedious, yet necessary work. If we wish to control the change we create in our life, it requires us to go above and beyond absentminded thinking. So, how would we go about doing just that?

Albert Einstein concluded that, "We cannot solve our problems with the same thinking we used when we created them." This has also been paraphrased to read, "No problem can be solved from the same level of consciousness that created it."

These two quotes combined give us the best insight into thinking differently.

Einstein's message means that to solve our problems or challenges, we need to upgrade our thinking to a level of perceptual awareness (consciousness) that provides different (new) views of our opportunities and problems, creating options. This means learning to see and study various other aspects of those situations without immediately judging them.

Thinking differently is hard work for the brain. This stems from the fact that our brains are actually lazy and would rather find a quick and easy solution by using shortcuts that require less effort. This approach allows the brain to conserve energy that can be utilized for the more significant occurrences in our lives.

On the positive side, this lazy, energy-saving approach to thinking has enabled man to invent hundreds of thousands of ideas over the centuries, which have advanced human development and changed the way we live.

Unfortunately, without a conscious effort to think differently, the vast majority of people continually try to solve their problems and challenges with the exact level of thinking they always have used; the same level of thinking at which the problem was created. We'll delve more deeply into the reasons for this in the chapters on decisions and habits.

Anyone who has had children knows how inquisitive a young child can be. They ask questions about everything. After they master the word "no" and expand their use of the language, who, what, when, where, why, and how became a few of their most common words in their vocabulary. Who is that? What is that? Where are we going? When will we get there? And the ultimate kid questions, why?

Their brains are like sponges, soaking up incredible amounts of information that they are processing and storing. To them, anything and everything is fair game for a question.

However, as they get older and begin the formal developmental learning process, moving them toward adulthood, they form thought patterns and opinions that conform with their environment and upbringing, which begins to curtail their open-mindedness. The result is that they begin to lose that inquisitive nature.

Then, their ego steps in, convincing them to believe the knowledge they have in certain areas is sufficient. Guarding and arguing for such beliefs becomes the ego's job.

Or, because of a desire for social acceptance, they become inhibited by concerns of what people think of them and they tend to stop asking those difficult to answer questions that challenge the status quo of their life.

As you can see, overcoming the ego and our habits of thought can be a very tall order. But understand this. It was your past and current way of thinking which got you to where you are now, like it or not. So, if you don't learn to think differently, you'll continue to struggle and get more of the same results.

In order to teach ourselves to think differently, we need to recapture that child-like desire and willingness to ask questions, especially the difficult ones.

The challenge is, as we are experiencing our day, how do we get ourselves to pause and mentally ask deeper questions such as: What is actually happening? What are the possible meanings? What might we think, say or do as a response? Why are we about to respond in a particular way?

Your goal should be to become more aware of those times when you are operating in an ego driven, judgmental unconsciousness and move into a higher level of consciousness that allows you to see and think differently.

But, be alert to the clever tactics the ego uses to maintain control of your mind. It will distract you from asking the challenging questions or convince you that your current understanding of and beliefs about the situation are sufficient. It is always looking to take over, again.

Posing challenging questions about what we think, say and do is not intended to disprove our beliefs, although that could occur. The intention is to find additional non-biased information that enables you to make more enlightened decisions. It's about keeping an open mind, creating awareness and developing a different level of conscious thinking that will better serve you in all areas of your life.

What happens when a new thought, which is in direct conflict with a strong belief, is introduced into your mind? Can you ask questions like: Could there be some truth to this thought? What might be true about it? Is it possible that my belief is not absolutely correct? What might not be true about my belief?

At one point in history, it was believed that the world was flat. This belief was sustained until men of the sciences began to question it and theorize that the world was actually round. I think you know the results of that science and history lesson. The point is, it took thinking differently to discover the truth.

An example in the world of sports, it was believed that the one mile run could not be completed in less than four minutes. It was thought that to do so would physically harm or kill the runner. A twenty-five year-old medical student from London, named Roger Bannister, thought differently about this widely believed limit. In 1954, he ran the first sub-four minute mile and changed the way future runners would view what was possible. Again, this was the result of thinking differently.

It's interesting to note that, today, college and high school runners are posting sub-four minute miles on a regular basis.

Let's relate this idea to you. Think about something in your life for which you held a strong belief that ultimately turned out to be not true.

To help you start thinking differently, we will encourage you to challenge many of the principles and concepts you have assumed to be true and put those things under the microscope of questioning. At the same time, open your mind to possibilities when you are listening to or reading information from other people.

Your mental capabilities are like the muscles in your body. If you work-out regularly, the muscles begin to develop and grow. Your brain and specifically your ability to think differently works the same way. And just like the muscle, the brain will atrophy if not given regular exercise, which explains why many people are where they are in their life today.

As you practice raising your level of awareness, keeping an open mind and asking yourself thought provoking questions, your ability to think differently will develop, laying the foundation for the change you will create.

Do this exercise regularly and you'll begin to have insights about people and tasks that will change your personal and work relationships.

ACTIVITY STEP

This activity is intended to help you learn to think differently by increasing your conscious awareness and eventually be able to do it without effort.

Warning: When you initially start using this exercise, it's best to avoid examining subjects like religion or politics. Such topics may cause some extreme cognitive resistance to completing or continuing this exercise.

Take 10 minutes to sit quietly at the start of each day. Think of a statement, action or idea of a co-worker or family member with which you disagreed. Write it down.

If you are having trouble thinking of something from a co-worker of family member, use one of your own statements, actions or ideas. Write out the exact opposite position, action or idea.

Now, mentally step back and with a child-like, curious mind, answer the following questions without applying your judgement. Give yourself permission to momentarily abandon your own beliefs and opinions.

How would I defend or justify this statement or action?

What could they be seeing that I don't see?

What about my viewpoint might not be completely true?

What are the benefits I get from disagreeing with the statement or action?

Is there another viewpoint that differs from their opinion and my opinion of the issue?

This is essentially a solo-brainstorming session. The strategy is to develop questions that create a different mental perspective from which to think.

Important note:

We'd like to re-emphasis a point. The intention of this activity is not to disprove or change your beliefs. It is to practice thinking differently. There is no right or wrong with this exercise. You are simply acknowledging opposite and different ideas, approaches or solutions, forcing yourself to think outside of YOUR mind.

Steve Jobs radically changed the digital music industry with the iPod on October 1, 2001. At a time when the majority of companies were trying to make a better MP3 player, he changed the dynamics by telling his engineers he wanted, "To be able to carry a thousand songs in his pocket." This, along with iTunes led to today's current Digital Music industry.

People like Thomas Edison, Nikola Tesla, Steve Jobs and Elon Musk were able to create innovative ideas that changed our world because they were able to think differently.

How could thinking differently change your world? I challenge you to make this practice a habit. Because, if you don't pick up anything else from this book, this practice can have a major impact on your life.

TAKE OWNERSHIP

> *"One of the points that all wise men*
> *and women agree on is this: If we*
> *want our world to improve, we should*
> *work on ourselves first. That's where*
> *the significant gains are to be found.*
> *Focusing on the inadequacies of*
> *others, or the unfairness in the world,*
> *is often just a trap of our own making*
> *as we resist looking in the mirror."*
> Joseph Deitch, Elevate:
> An Essential Guide to Life

When good things happen in our life, most of us are usually quick to attribute the good fortune to our own efforts. We'll think, "I nailed that interview. He offered me the promotion on the spot. He obviously recognizes great talent." And in fact, as we will see, we did have a major impact on what happened.

But when things don't go as we'd like them to, we are just as quick to assign blame or justify our misfortunes and failures to achieve the results we wanted. "My boss doesn't know what he's doing. I can't believe he chose that block-head over me for the promotion."

If we are going to create the change we want to see, we will first need to take ownership of everything that comes into our life.

In the context of this book, taking ownership refers to the process of owning who you are, personally and professionally, and the state of your life in all areas. It's accepting personal responsibility for how you've developed and for what you have (or don't have) in your life.

TWO VITAL AREAS IN WHICH TO TAKE RESPONSIBILITY.

The first area are the things we can control; our thoughts, our feelings, the words we speak and the actions we take. The reason these areas are important is because they are the main ingredients in creating the results we get in life. That is, your thoughts, feelings, words, and actions of today will determine the person you become and the life you will have tomorrow.

The second area in which we need to take responsibility is for things that happen to us over which we have no control. I'm referring to the accidents, unfortunate occurrences, and situations that block our development or, completely alter our life. How we handle these misfortunes is also a major determinant of the results in our life.

Some of you are thinking, "What? I'm supposed to take responsibility for an accident that happened to me?" Yes, but we're not entirely referring to assigning blame for the incident happening. While you may actually have contributed to the cause of the occurrence, I'm referring to taking responsibility for what you will do next.

Look, taking ownership or responsibility for what happens in our life is not an easy task. This is evident by the fact that personal responsibility is an uncommon practice in the world. The "It's not my fault" attitude shows up everywhere. The news is constantly running stories about business executives, civic leaders and politicians pointing the finger of blame at their competitor, adversary, or a convenient scapegoat when things go wrong in areas governed by their authority.

And it's not just the high-profile people. There are many individuals at every level of society who don't think they have to accept responsibility for the results in their life. And if you watch and listen carefully at work or at home, I'm certain you will hear it there, too. You may even recognize it in yourself.

People are more inclined to look outside of themselves for the reasons for who they have become, why they don't have what they want, or why things went wrong. It is far easier to make excuses or blame circumstances or other people for the negative events happening in their life. No effort is required to give up in situations when they have been dealt a bad hand, rather than stop and look at how they could find seeds of a benefit in their challenge and what they could do next to get back in control of their life.

As you will learn, nothing just "happens." According to the Principle of Cause and Effect, one of the primary postulates that govern how our world works states, "that every event is an effect and has another event as a cause and is itself the cause of yet another effect (think chain reaction). The principle also maintains that there is no such thing as chance, an uncaused happening."

This means that everything in our experience, everything in the Universe, is the direct result of some prior event or action that was the *cause* of the results we observe. Everything.

Unfortunately, few people grasp this. Many attempt to direct their lives, looking at the "effect" in a given situation, rather than the cause. We see this played out over and over in society.

But before we move on, we want to emphasis an important point. Self-responsibility is not about blaming ourselves. Self-blame is a useless activity and the associated guilt is a wasted emotion. Together, they keep us stuck in a cycle of helplessness. In that state, taking charge of our self-responsibility becomes extremely difficult.

When we talk about self-responsibility, we're also referring to control of our life through self-empowerment and self-control. You see, when we make excuses and blame other people and circumstances for who we are or what we have and don't have, we are giving up control of our life and our power. We are saying that someone or something else other than ourselves are in control and dictating the results we have received in our life.

The truth is, who we are and what is going on in our lives are direct results ((the effect) of several areas of cause: the beliefs we individually hold (true or false), the decisions we make or don't make (positive or negative) and the habits we form (constructive or destructive).

Certainly, our ability to take ownership is affected by how we manage these vital mental elements in our mind. They will be covered in greater depth in upcoming chapters and hopefully help solidify the change we will begin here.

Here, I want to create an awareness and begin to help you learn to assume responsibility for you and where you are, to stop placing blame on other people or circumstances or life in general, and to not accepting the bad situation or event that occur in your life. The sooner you can take control, the sooner you will be able to manifest significant change for yourself and others.

Of all the things you're learning to adopt, this one might be the hardest. Accepting responsibility can be painful, a sensation we typically avoid. And recognizing that we have a choice to pick ourselves up and pursue our dreams after a personal disaster, takes an incredible amount of courage, faith and resolve.

This is an especially tough pill to swallow if one has formed the habits of complaining, blaming, defending, justifying and projecting, and can't or won't understand what we are discussing here. It is this type of continuous self-deception which makes it extremely difficult to take ownership of our life.

THE UNMANAGED EGO

As you attempt to take responsibility for your life, the unmanaged ego will be extremely resistant to this thinking. The lack of self-responsibility and the willingness to blame others are hallmarks of an unmanaged ego. In its efforts to protect us, help us feel good about ourselves, and prevent us from looking bad in the eyes of others, it will continually give us reasons to explain our situation and problems, to deflect any responsibility for why we are struggling or are faced with challenges.

People think: It's my wife's or my husband's fault because she/ he made me angry. This is all my boss or my co-workers fault because they didn't tell me I needed to do that task. It's my parents fault that I'm struggle with this issue, they don't understand me. It's my coaches fault because she doesn't like me.

The problem becomes more ingrained in us as we subconsciously form the habit of projecting blame for our circumstances on something or someone else. This type of behavior positions us as victims in our mind and gives further justification for abdicating our power of self-responsibility. It takes a willingness and confidence to confront our ego and force it to be our servant rather than the other way around.

If we are to create the change we want to see, we'll also need to look at that second area in which we must learn to take ownership of our lives: Those instances where things were out of our control; the accidents, illnesses and catastrophes that may give us many reasons to give up on ourselves. How can we take ownership under those circumstances? Let's look at the story of a man named W. Mitchell.

One day, Mitchell, who was a cable car grip-man in San Francisco, was riding to his job on his new motorcycle. As he proceeded through an intersection, a commercial truck ran a stop sign, broadsiding him. The impact sent Mitchell and his motorcycle skidding across the street. But worse yet, it caused the gas cap of the motorcycle to pop open, releasing several gallons of gasoline onto Mitchell. The sparks from the motorcycle sliding on the surface ignited the gasoline, and instantly he was engulfed in flames. With burns over 65% of his body, he lost most of his 10 fingers and his face was burned beyond recognition. His life plans had been drastically altered with no clear direction other than survival.

Through four long years of pain, extensive surgeries and therapy, Mitchell began to reconstruct his life. He decided that he wanted to return to flying small aircraft, something he had started to do shortly before the accident and an activity that was one of his great pleasures in life.

On a rather cold day, as he prepared for take-off for a casual flight, he had not detected a thin layer of ice on the wings of the aircraft, a condition which can dramatically affect stability of an aircraft taking flight. As he sped down the runway and started to rise from the ground, he lost control of the plane and it crashed. In an effort to escape the wreckage, he realized that he couldn't move his legs. The impact had damaged his spine, paralyzing him from the waist down.

Unfortunately, the injury was not able to be repaired. He would now be confined to a wheelchair.

He kept asking himself, "Why me? Why me? How could fate be so cruel? Not once, but twice." These events were far more than most of us could ever deal with. If ever anyone had a reason to give up, it was probably Mitchell. He dealt with every negative emotion you could imagine.

But one day, he came to grips with his responsibility for the situation. He realized that he could not change one thing about what had already happened to him. The only thing he had any control over was how he would deal with his life going forward. He decided that he would stop being the victim, looking at all the things he could no longer do. He chose to look for the things that he *could* do.

It was this thinking that launched him into a speaking career with a goal to change people's perspective about life challenges. His message was that we will all find ourselves in tough situations as we travel through life. It could be related to health, finances, relationships or career. While most of the situations we experience won't be as challenging as Mitchell's, we must find the strength to take responsibility for what we will do to move ourselves beyond those situations.

The key takeaway here is that while it was not his thoughts, words and actions that created the situations he found himself in, it would be his new thoughts, words and actions that would enable him to take ownership of his life and the change that he wanted to create.

Look at the current state of your life right now. Perhaps it isn't what you'd hoped it would be. Perhaps you are struggling to overcome challenges (maybe it's you). Can you see how consciously choosing your thoughts, words, and actions, in the current moment, empowers you to take ownership of your life and positions you to create the change you want to see?

ACTIVITY STEP - INTERNALIZING

To start this exercise, refer back to the chapter on awareness. This will be the foundation for taking ownership. As you become more aware of your thinking, feelings, words and actions, you give yourself the opportunity to more closely examine them.

Next, think of areas of your life or unachieved goals with which you are struggling or not getting the results you want. It could be in your health, finances, relationships, education or career. Write down three.

For each, list the thoughts, conversations, or actions which are portraying you as a victim, subverting your ownership of the situation, or abdicating your power to take action.

Then, for each self-defeating behavior/message, write a positive, counter thought or action that you will use to assume responsibility and to take ownership.

For example, let's say you admit that you are struggling to hit a sales goal which your company has assigned to you. The subversive activities you Identify could be something like: a) you think other sales people received better territories, b) you complain to friends about how unfair your manager is to you, c) you find other work activities to do rather than make sales calls.

Your counter actions could be: a) you begin reviewing all of the accounts in your territory with whom you are not yet doing business, b) you create a list of all of the ways your manager supports your sales effort, c) you focus on sales calls before any other activities and do 10% more than required.

As you begin to do this exercise, watch out for the defensive thoughts produced by your ego. It will likely resist doing this exercise. Remind yourself that you do have a choice to take control. Just keep asking yourself the tough questions.

> "The mere formulation of a problem
> is far more often essential than
> its solution, which may be merely
> a matter of mathematical or
> experimental skill. To raise new
> questions, new possibilities, to regard
> old problems from a new angle
> requires creative imagination and
> marks real advances in science."
> Albert Einstein

MAKING THE COMMITMENT
TO CHANGE

Ultimately, this book is about changing our lives for the better. But, the prospect of significant life change scares most of us. That's because making a commitment to change means leaving your comfort zone and pushing yourself to take actions that may be challenging or risky. But the goal is not just to become comfortable with change, it is to actually learn to embrace change in order to leverage it to our advantage. If you will commit to change and practice being a change agent, success will come looking for you

People in the 85% category, mentioned earlier, are set in their ways and find it difficult to change. Yes, they want good things to come into their lives, but they are unwilling or unable to first do the hard work of changing themselves, a necessary step in the process.

It's completely normal for people of all ages to talk about the change they'd like to make to better their lives. Young children talk about what they want to be when they grow up. Teenagers talk about the career path they will pursue. Young adults talk about the new job they interviewed for. Middle aged people talk about moving up the ranks of their company or getting more responsibility and money with their next job move. People at every phase of life are dreaming of some next goal that enables them to live better, more comfortably.

We seem to have a sense that we can achieve more and do greater things in our life. This sense of possibility is the seeds of greatness that our Creator has placed in each and every one of us. We are His greatest creation and He has high hopes for us.

This is a subconscious yearning that can be fueled and nurtured, or stifled and crushed, depending on the people we meet, the actions we take, the success or failures we have and how our minds process all of these experiences.

If you are fortunate, you've had people in your life who encourage and support you in the pursuit of your goals. You may have had experiences that helped build the confidence to keep moving forward in the face of difficulty.

However, as we progress through life and the things we want require greater effort and greater risk, people begin to ignore or stifle their own desires. They listen to well-intended friends and family who discourage them from exploring their greatness because it might be risky for their future or it's just not practical. Because of negative mental programming of their mind, they question their ability to achieve that goal.

And, that is another reason for this book. We want it to be a catalyst for your personal growth, to motivate you to go after those tough goals even in the face of doubt and negativity, and then for you to become a catalyst for others.

We are asking you to define specifically what you want in any or all areas of your life. Decide which of those big, audacious goals lingering in the recesses of your mind you will focus on; those thoughts of greatness that you have been suppressing.

The discussion of goal setting covered in this book is just to provide a frame of reference for the core messages. We will go beyond goal setting to explore areas that affect your ability to achieve your goals, objectives, and desires such as your beliefs, decisions, and habits.

To reach the goals you choose, you will also have to make an additional decision to learn and use the information you receive in those areas, and other principles in this book.

To help facilitate this, we'll ask you to make some commitments, to dedicate and obligate yourself to a set of goals in your life, and to utilize the principles in this book. Those are definitely impactful words: *dedicate* and *obligate*. If you truly want change, if you truly want to reach goals that will stretch you to become a greater person, to tap into your potential, you will have to make a serious commitment.

Hopefully as you learn about your beliefs, decisions and habits, and how they work, you'll see how they can support your objectives or restrict your progress toward them. With this understanding and the principles previously discussed, you will realize amazing results.

In support of our readers and followers, we have created a Facebook Community to provide a place where like-minded people can share thoughts, strategies and wins, exchange and explore ideas, ask questions, provide encouragement and even some accountability. You can join this community by going to:

Join Us on Facebook
(https://www.facebook.com/groups/CreateTheChange/)

VINCE PAPALE'S STORY
BY SKI SWIATKOWSKI

Before we dive into the elements of our beliefs, decisions and habits, let's look at someone who has actually used these to create the change they wanted to see in their life.

Perhaps one of the best examples of this is my good friend, Vince Papale. You may be familiar with Vince through a book called, *Invincible*: My Journey from Fan to NFL Team Captain. His amazing experience became a 2006 Disney movie, starring Mark Wahlberg in the leading role.

The story line was about the unlikely prospect of a 30-year-old Philadelphia Eagles fan, who played only one year of high school football and had absolutely no college football experience, trying out and actually making the roster of a National Football League team, his beloved Eagles. It sounds like an unbelievable fairytale made up for the movies, doesn't it? But except for a few historic details left out of the movie storyline to increase the Wow factor, he really did what the vast majority of people believed was impossible.

When I first met Vince, his story was already unfolding. We were teammates on a semi-professional football team called the Philadelphia-Aston Knights. (This was a portion of his journey that was omitted from the Invincible movie.)

The Knights were an interesting group of guys, who were beyond their high school and college playing days, but wanted to continue being part of the game they loved. Some of these players had been released from the NFL and Canadian Football League teams and were looking to get another chance. Some were like me, dreamers who were a bit too small and too slow to make it in the NFL.

Then, there were a few exceptional guys, who had aspirations and the raw potential to make it in the highly competitive NFL. They just needed the chance to prove themselves. Vince was one of these people.

Coming out of high school, there was no question Vince was an incredible athlete. He had received a full scholarship to run track at St. Joseph's University, where he further developed his natural speed.

Playing for the Philadelphia-Aston Knights brought Vince together with an outstanding quarterback by the name of John Waller, who still holds many of Temple University's passing records and is in their hall of fame.

Together, Vince and John tore up the Seaboard League, leading all statistics in passing and receiving. Those two were a huge part of the success the Knights experienced. People in the Philadelphia area began to notice and talk about Vince Papale. Friends and Knights head coach, Phil Pompilli, attempted to help Vince contact the Eagles to get a tryout, but messages to the Eagles went unanswered. He had heard comments that he'd never make the NFL, that he wasn't good enough. But he made a **decision** to give those comments a different meaning. He chose to use them as fuel for his desire and to prove the naysayers wrong.

Then, in 1974, a new opportunity would appear for Vince. It was an upstart rival to the NFL called the World Football League. As chance would have it, Philadelphia was given a franchise which was named the Bell, obviously referring to the Liberty Bell, which is part of the city's history and the symbol of United States independence.

The tryout for the Philadelphia Bell drew over 500 athletes. With almost 70 men trying out at wide receiver, Vince's position. The competition was fierce. But when the coaches saw his speed and ability to catch a football, he was a lock for a spot on the team.

As a member of the Bell, Vince had the chance to display his talent on a national stage. He was a steady contributor as a wide receiver and a standout on special teams.

Unfortunately, the World Football League folded after only one and a half seasons of operation. Vince was out of football, but the experience with the Bell affirmed his confidence in his ability and desire to play professional football. His **belief** in himself continued to grow.

Then, through a turn of events, fate smiled down on Vince once again. In 1976, the Philadelphia Eagles changed head coaches, hiring a highly-regarded college coach named Dick Vermeil. An aggressive thinker, Vermeil wanted to try new strategies and approaches. In a bit of a public relations move, he decided to hold a tryout open to anyone interested in making the team.

With his Aston Knight and Philadelphia Bell experience under his belt, Vince attended the open tryouts. It was this experience, his tremendous speed and ability, and certainly his growing **belief** in himself that enabled Vince to stand out from all of the other athletes there. His performance caught the attention of the Eagles coaching staff to such a degree that the Eagles management offered him a player contract and an invitation to training camp with the team.

It was incredible that he had made it this far. The possibility of his dream of playing in the NFL was getting closer to becoming real. But his biggest challenge was in front of him; to survive the cuts of training camp and to officially be named to the Eagles player roster.

An important **decision** Vince made in the off-season prior to training camp was to work out with the quarterbacks at the team's practice facility. He was the only wide receiver to attend these practices, including the veteran players. From these sessions, he drew great encouragement from important members of the team, like quarterback Roman Gabriel, as well as some coaches.

Training camp brought with it another challenge; getting the other players and the coaches to believe in Vince. After all, here was this thirty year-old rookie, who didn't play college football, who didn't have the resume, who didn't go through the expected path to the NFL. He saw blatant and disguised resentment. They rode him on the field and in the locker room. But as Vince told me, he made the **decision** to not let the jealousy, insecurities, pettiness and doubts of others steal his dream. He made the choice to "focus" on what he needed to do to make the dream happen.

One **habit** that Vince formed that got the coaches to notice him was to give extra effort when he caught a pass in practice and scrimmages. Normally, a wide receiver will catch a pass, stop and return to the group, mostly to conserve energy through the practice. Not Vince. He would run another 50-60 yards after catching a pass. The local fans, who attended training camp sessions, would go crazy. They loved their hometown hero. It was as if he were living their fantasy for them.

Needless to say, this didn't endear him to some of the other players. But the coaches did notice and liked his hustle and drive. He continued the **habit** of giving that extra effort every time he stepped on the field.

After training camp had started and they moved into the pre-season games, Vince had the opportunity to participate in live action against NFL opposition. He took full advantage of these. His performance demonstrated to both the coaches and the other players that he could make the right reads of the defense, adjust, and make great plays. They began to accept him more and more. He was winning their respect and his dream was moving closer to reality.

Finally, the day of final player cuts arrived, when all NFL teams had to reduce their rosters to the 53-man limit. When the cut list was announced to the media, Vince Papale was not on it! He was officially a member of the Philadelphia Eagles! He achieved his dream in spite of all of the challenges he faced. It was his beliefs, his decisions, and his habits along the journey that ultimately made it happen.

Vince went on to play 3 seasons with the Eagles before a shoulder injury ended his career. A regular part of the receiver corps, he was named Special Teams Captain in 1978 by his teammates and "Man of the Year" for his involvement with charities.

Since the *Invincible* book and movie, Vince has co-authored two other books and is a highly sought-after public speaker.

I've given you a glimpse of how "Mr. Invincible" used his beliefs, decisions and habits to turn his dream of playing in the NFL into reality. He created the change that he wanted to see and continues to show others how to do it as well.

As we continue to explore the key elements of change: Your Beliefs, Decisions, and Habits, keep Vince's journey in mind. While you are probably not looking to play in the NFL, you will likely encounter challenges on your own journey. Vince's story will give a perspective of how tough and yet rewarding the effort can be.

Besides being my friend, Vince has been an inspiration to me on the journey to my dream to writing and speaking my message. When we got together to chat about his story and his part in this book, he told me one of his favorite quotes. He said: "Happy are those who dream dreams and are ready to pay the price to make them come true."

Your dreams are the Change You Want to See. Part of paying the price is learning the process of Creating that Change. The other ingredient to make dreams come true, is your action.

WHATEVER YOU BELIEVE

BY JIM DONOVAN

From books like James Allen's *As a Man Thinketh* (1906), and Thomas Troward's *Edinburg Lectures* (1906) to Napoleon Hill's "Think and Grow *Rich*" (1936) and Claude Bristol›s *Magic of Believing* (1945), to the very book you're reading, the subject of beliefs has been written about in every self-help, personal development, and success book ever written.

It is that important

A belief is any thought, idea or concept we accept as a fact, anything we assume to be true. Resting in our sub-conscious mind, they give us the ability to make decisions and judgements that help us navigate our way through everyday life.

We usually form our beliefs in two ways: a) by our experiences and the conclusions we reach based on evidence and reasoning, and b) from the acceptance of what others tell us to be the truth.

WHERE BELIEFS ORIGINATE

At birth, we come into the world with no beliefs. We are similar to a new computer with a blank memory. As we see, hear, touch, smell and taste things, we begin to record and compare the data we are accumulating. In those early years, it is the interaction with our parents and our environment that most shape our beliefs.

As our development continues, we receive input from well-intentioned people in our lives; our teachers, ministers, family members, peers, even society in general. Prior to reaching the age of reason (approximately years 6 or 7), our ability to decide what is true or not true, what is correct or incorrect thinking, has not yet fully developed. Our minds are being conditioned by these sources with information we automatically accept as true.

This base mental conditioning can result in beliefs that either support or undermine a child's ability to grow into a well-balanced, happy adult. Thus, it is through this conditioning where the potential for many problems begin.

Early-stage mental conditioning is the primary cause behind discrimination towards groups of people. Most of those who hate members of a particular group, do so based on information they were taught to believe as children.

It is also at the root of the problems we have with combating terrorism. We are dealing with people who were conditioned during their childhood to hate others whose beliefs are different from theirs. Essentially, they've been brainwashed with those beliefs.

The problem is, for the most part, those well-intentioned adults were simply repeating beliefs that were handed down from the adults who raised them. We have what my colleague, David Neagle, author of "The Millions Within: How to Manifest Exactly What You Want" (Morgan James Publishing 2013), refers to as "Multi-generational dysfunction." We have generations of people passing on their beliefs that, in many cases, are not true.

One of my most empowering practices is found in an article from decades ago that examined our beliefs and prejudices. The author suggested, that as adults we owe it to ourselves to examine what we were told to believe about the world when we were children, and decide if now, from our adult perspective, we still agree with them.

For instance, just because my family chose to believe something about a group of people does not mean that I, as an adult, want to believe it.

A young child, raised with racist beliefs, has the power as an adult to question those beliefs, examine the information pertaining to them and decide if they are valid or not.

Keep in mind how many beliefs people held as truth, in some cases for hundreds of years, that turned out to be simply beliefs and had nothing to do with the truth. "The world is flat" and "man was not meant to fly," are just two beliefs that were accepted as true in their day.

DEFENDING YOUR LIMITING BELIEFS

If you listen carefully to the conversations of people, you'll notice that their words will reveal their limiting beliefs. Learn to pay close attention to the thoughts and words you repeatedly tell yourself over and over again about your abilities. Try to identify your own limiting beliefs. They are sabotaging your success, often without you even being aware it's happening.

Here's a tip. When you hear yourself, or someone else, say something like, "I can't _____ (whatever it is you desire) *because* _____". Whatever follows the word *because* is usually the limiting belief.

WE ALL HAVE A STORY

In order to live with the limiting belief, we make up stories that support it and repeat these stories to ourselves and others, again and again. You have told "your story" enough times that you now believe it to be true.

Just because we believe something to be true, does not make it so. Just because the majority of people believe a particular viewpoint (a global belief), does not make it a fact.

As we continuously repeat a particular idea in our internal and external conversations, our mind begins to accept it as true, though it often is not. This is how limiting beliefs are planted and cultivated in the mind.

The limiting or disempowering belief strengthens to a point where we defend it as though it is somehow sacred, never to be challenged. We may even become angry or resentful of anyone else who dares to question our belief, even though challenging the belief is exactly what we need to be doing.

A very interesting fact about beliefs is, once a belief is challenged and disproven, it dissolves and no longer exists. We've seen this happening on the world stage in recent history. A long-held belief among Americans was that an African-American could never be elected as president. Barack Obama disproved this in 2008 by being elected President of the United States. Once this happened, the belief was shattered by fact.

You read earlier about Roger Bannister becoming the first person to break the four-minute mile; something that no one for two thousand years was able to do! What's fascinating about this event is that within a month of his doing it, some thirty-people accomplished the same feat. And in 2011, a Norwegian 16-year-old, Jakob Ingebritsen, became the youngest runner to break four minutes for the mile.

Consider, for a moment, that throughout history no one was able to run a mile in less than four minutes until one single person accomplished it. Once the belief was destroyed, it became possible for others to do the same.

What changed? Did people's physical abilities improve? Possibly, to a small extent, their strength and endurance improved, but it was more a result of disproving the limiting belief, which was never a fact in the first place. What actually changed in this scenario was the belief held by a single person that it was possible.

It is important to note, however, that Bannister did not simply change his belief, he also took massive action and trained hard for the event.

SUCCESS AND YOUR LIMITING BELIEFS

As we mentioned earlier, the subject of beliefs is one of the key concepts in creating a more successful life.

If there is one thing that will stop you from ever accomplishing what you're meant to do in your life, it is the limiting beliefs you have about yourself and your abilities.

A limiting or disempowering belief will keep you stuck right where you are. They are, perhaps, the greatest hurdles to your accomplishing what you desire in your life. Until you alter whatever particular beliefs are standing in the way of your success, nothing is going to change.

What you believe about yourself and your abilities will set the stage for everything you do or even attempt to do. If, for example, you're carrying around a deep-seated belief that you'll never get ahead in life, you will continually act out that belief in your everyday experience.

A business person who believes that they are not good in sales will make a half-hearted effort in selling and, as a result, not produce the results they desire. Their belief in not being good at sales will creep into their thinking to sabotage any effort they do make. With insufficient effort, they will struggle and fail. This will further confirm the belief that's keeping them trapped and the story continues.

In truth, their lack of sales ability is more likely a lack of proper training and preparation, not a fact. Contrary to popular thinking, great salespeople are not born that way. If you take the time to study successful sales people, you will see that similar to any profession, they trained, studied and prepared until they acquired a proficiency in sales.

Their success is the result of their beliefs, decisions and habits, not some inborn talent they were blessed with. Both Ski and I have worked with enough salespeople throughout our careers to know this to be a fact.

JIM'S LESSON IN THE POWER OF BELIEFS

In the early stages of my career life, I worked in broadcast television. I began initially as a Broadcast Engineer working first at the ABC television network in

New York and then at the Hughes Sports Network, which is now the MSG Network.

Though I was assigned as an editor to the videotape center, I would occasionally be asked to report to Madison Square garden to fill-in as a cameraman for an event there. One particular evening as I exited the subway at Penn Station, I saw several large trucks marked, "Ringling Bros. Barnum & Bailey Circus," parked along eighth avenue and realized the circus was in town.

Since I always enjoyed going to the circus as a child, I became excited at the possibility of going backstage. Because I worked there, I was not subject to the restrictions placed on the general public and was free to go wherever I wanted in the building. I decided to spend my dinner hour exploring the circus preparation activities; something most people are unable to do.

It was fascinating to be behind the scenes at "The Greatest Show on Earth," the name they used to promote it. I walked along the Rotunda, the area around the performance arena, passing a variety of circus animals along the way. I passed lions, tigers, giraffes, and the beautiful Lipizzaner stallions.

Further along I saw a line of elephants, ranging in size from the small, young baby elephants to the fully-grown adults. Each were held in place by a single strand of rope around the bottom of one leg, which was tied to a stake in the dirt.

Looking at this I was dumbfounded. How was it that these giant, majestic animals were being held by a small rope tied to a stake in the ground? For starters, the large elephants could certainly break free from the rope anytime they wanted. Secondly, since the arena at MSG is five stories above the ground, the dirt was only several inches deep, put there to accommodate the circus.

I went over to the trainer and asked why the elephants didn't simply walk away. He proceeded to tell me that when the elephants are quite small and unable to break the rope, they were tied to a tree. (Please note: I do not condone this terrible treatment of animals.)

He went on to explain that the young elephant would try to break free, but was unable to do so. After some time, the elephant would just give-up. In psychology, this is referred to as "learned helplessness." The baby elephant grows up *believing* there's nothing it can do when it has a rope tied to its leg.

WHAT ARE YOUR ROPES (LIMITING BELIEFS)?

So, what are the limiting beliefs you're carrying around, that are holding you back from becoming the person you want to be and living the life of your dreams?

We'll revisit this in an "Activity" later but, for now, start thinking about those things you tell yourself that prevent you from creating the change in your life that will manifest those dreams.

HOW YOUR BELIEFS AFFECT YOUR EVERYDAY LIFE

Here's how your beliefs affect your day-to-day life. When something new enters your awareness through your conscious mind, it is immediately filtered by your subconscious beliefs about whatever it is, along with your past conditioning, and memories of similar events.

CHANGING YOUR LIMITING BELIEFS

The good news is, that the latest brain research teaches us that, with enough positive self-talk and positive visualization, combined with training, coaching and practice, anyone can change their beliefs and learn to do almost anything they desire.

ATTITUDE IS EVERYTHING

In order to accomplish something you've never done before, it is essential for you to change your attitude from "I can't" to "I can and will," regardless of your past results.

Many of us were not raised with much positivity or provided with empowering beliefs to support us and our abilities. As a result, most people, "Live lives of quiet desperation," as stated by Thoreau.

Personally, I find this quite sad and have devoted the past twenty-five years of my life to writing, speaking and coaching people who want to change their circumstances and have a better life. Regardless of where you are right now in your life, you *can* change. You have within you the power to change your life and rewrite your own personal story.

I was one of those people who didn't receive much positive support as I grew up. My grandfather did a great job of teaching me how to ice skate, swim, shoot, and fish. But when it came to encouraging me to believe in myself, he took the exact opposite approach. I remember one day, in an effort to motivate me, he said, "You're a lazy bum just like your father and will never amount to anything." Needless to say, it depressed me and had the reverse effect from what it was intended to accomplish. I just became that much more dysfunctional.

This is just the way it was back then and is still true today. There are many people who believe the way to help someone improve was to belittle them into trying harder. We now know this does not work. It never did and never will. Granted, it will produce a result and may even appear to work for a time, but in the long run, berating someone to do better is like hitting your computer with a hammer to make it perform faster; something you'd never think of doing. Why then do we do it with those we care about?

Fortunately, as I got older and began my own search for my life's meaning, I learned there are better ways to increase and improve performance. This is one of the reasons I've been a student of personal development for more than thirty years. I have read more than five hundred books, attended countless seminars, and listened to and viewed numerous audio and video programs and continue to do so today.

I have learned I can change anything I want about myself by changing my thinking, attitude, beliefs, habits and decisions about who I am and what I am capable of. I have written more than eight books, which have been translated into a dozen languages and are available in twenty-six countries. Several of these have been international best-sellers, with hundreds of thousands of copies sold. This is a result of strengthening my beliefs, training myself to make better decisions, and forming habits that aid my successes.

BREAKING THROUGH YOUR LIMITING BELIEFS

There are several ways you can change or eliminate your limiting beliefs. The techniques range from simply questioning whether or not they're true, to using affirmations and visualization techniques, to replacing the limiting thoughts with powerful, positive statements that support beliefs that will serve you.

You can employ energy healing techniques like EFT (Emotional Freedom Technique), described below, and similar tools that interrupt the energy patterns in your body and help to release the belief.

IDENTIFYING THE BELIEFS THAT ARE STOPPING YOU

To break through your limiting beliefs, the first thing you need to do is recognize what they are. In your notebook or journal, list one or two beliefs about each of the various areas of your life: social, career, financial, spiritual, physical and material that are preventing you from being, doing or having the things you desire and deserve.

What are you consistently telling yourself about your ability, or lack thereof, in those areas? Write them down.

BELIEFS ARE LIKE A THREE-LEGGED STOOL

One of the reasons we continue to maintain a belief, even though it is clearly not serving us, is because we have developed references that give credibility to it.

Think of a person who considers themselves a good dancer. They've been collecting references that enable them to accept that belief. Perhaps, when they were young, someone commented that they were a good dancer. This became one of the "legs" supporting their belief. And like the legs of a stool, it served to reinforce the belief, whether or not it's actually true.

We also develop our own references that reinforce our beliefs. The young child who is carrying around a belief that they're not good at sports will make a half-hearted attempt and give up quickly, saying something like, "See? I knew I wasn't good at this."

While their poor performance is more likely the result of not having properly learned and developed the needed skills, they're convinced that they are not cut out for sports. Another "leg" has been put in place to support that belief. Then, they accept that as fact, and never make another attempt to participate in it.

IS THIS BELIEF REALLY TRUE?

As mentioned, you can begin to breakdown limiting beliefs with a simple question. Ask yourself, "Is this belief really 100% true?" After closely examining the belief and various aspects of it, you'll often realize it's not completely true. Perhaps, it's not at all true.

When you question a belief, the very act of questioning begins to weaken it. Using our three-legged stool example, questioning the belief is akin to knocking out one of the supporting "legs" that are holding it in place.

As you continue to question the different characteristics of your limiting beliefs, you are in effect weakening it until there are no longer references for its support. At this point, the belief no longer has power over your thinking.

FIND REFERENCES TO DISPROVE YOUR BELIEF AND SUPPORT YOUR DESIRES

For example, supposing your desire is to start your own business. It is something you'd really like to do. However, you're also harboring a deep-seated belief that you cannot succeed in business because you didn't graduate college.

Ask if there is anyone you know of, or have read about, who have started and succeeded in business in spite of their lack of formal education. I can almost guarantee you will learn about people, probably right in your own city or town, who have been successful in their own business and do not have a college degree.

The truth is, many entrepreneurs and successful business owners did quite poorly in school. Typically, the type of person who launches a successful business is not the best student. The inherent nature of the entrepreneur is to think outside the box and they're generally at odds with the rules and structure necessary to excel in school.

AFFIRMATIONS AND VISUALIZATION TECHNIQUES TO BREAKTHROUGH LIMITING BELIEFS

As you have learned, your limiting beliefs have been created in your mind through the mental recording of non-supportive messages from various sources. The result is similar to data input being written on the memory of a computer. While the limiting beliefs may be embedded in your mind, you have the ability to overwrite them with a more positive statement.

The idea is to input a new empowering command (the affirmation) that, over time, will replace the limiting belief.

Business guru, Brian Tracy, teaches sales people to repeat over and over prior to any sales call, "I'm a great salesperson." Doing this will help you focus on your success and helps to block out your "Monkey Mind" and internal dialog that is sabotaging your effort.

DESIGNING AFFIRMATIONS TO SUPPORT YOU

In order to ensure your affirmations are effective, follow these simple suggestions:

Phrase your affirmations in the positive

Since your subconscious mind thinks in pictures, not words, it does not recognize negative commands using words such as, "No" or "Not." For example, try "not" thinking of an elephant. What is conjured in your mind, of course, the image of an elephant.

Therefore, it is important to state affirmations in a positive, visual way that focus on what you want, rather than what you are trying to eliminate or avoid. So, instead of saying something like, "I am not going to gain weight," rephrase it to a statement, such as "I am feeling great being at my ideal weight of 165 pounds."

Phrase them in the present tense

Saying "I will" be, do or have something in particular is not as effective as stating it in the present tense. The words "I am" or "I have" are the strongest words you can use to begin your affirmation. It is declarative and signals your subconscious mind that you are serious.

Engage your emotions

Emotion is an instinctive state of mind that has a major impact on our behavior. When creating an affirmation, use words that express passion. By repeating an affirmation that is charged with emotion, it increases the intensity of the message to the brain. Gradually, it begins to accept the affirmation as fact and behavioral change follows.

SEE YOURSELF AS THE PERSON YOU WANT TO BECOME

Devoting a little time each day to visualize your desires is one of the best ways to start to create your new life. Since your subconscious mind cannot tell the difference between that which is true and that which is vividly imagined with feeling, you can effectively "trick" yourself into seeing a more successful you.

The more time you spend engaging your emotions and feelings, while visualizing your desires, the faster you will attract them to you. Visualization will improve your self-image.

If you want to feel more confident. Walk with confidence. Talk confidently. Imagine yourself in situations where you exhibit confidence.

TAPPING AWAY YOUR LIMITING BELIEFS AND MORE

A technique that has become very popular in recent years, with several documentaries and books detailing the topic, is a "Tapping" technique known as Emotional Freedom Technique (EFT).

EFT is a meridian based therapy developed by Gary Craig, based on the landmark discoveries of Dr. Richard Callahan. Dr. Callahan discovered that a person's fears, phobias, and other undesirable mental states could be treated by tapping on specific acupressure meridians.

I have personally been trained in EFT and have used it successfully on myself and with family members, often with remarkable results. Leading edge therapists are using EFT in conjunction with traditional modalities because of its ability to produce rapid results. Much of Craig's early work was in treating returning Vietnam War veterans suffering from a variety of traumas.

Today, there is the *Veterans Stress Project* (www. stressproject.org), part of the National Institute for Integrative Healthcare (NIIH), offering help for veterans, especially those suffering with PTSD. They are having amazing results. One multi-year study of veterans with PTSD resulted in a *60% reduction in symptoms* as a result of the EFT treatments. And the Veterans Stress Project found that 8 out of 10 veterans, who came to the site for help, and completed 6 one-hour EFT treatments, no longer tested positive for PTSD. With veterans-suicide at an all-time high, this is significant.

The basic premise of EFT is that the cause of all negative emotion is a disruption in the body's energy system. The technique itself involves simply repeating a phrase that describes the problem, while at the same time, tapping a sequence of acupressure points on the body. I realize this sounds overly simple; however, I have personally witnessed extraordinary results.

Our limiting beliefs function similarly to fears and phobias in that they produce negative emotional responses when they've been triggered. By using this tapping technique on limiting beliefs, you can weaken the belief, if not eliminate it altogether.

If you'd like to know more about this, our resource page has links to several of the leading sources of EFT information.

STRENGTHENING YOUR EMPOWERING BELIEFS

Now that you've started weakening and eliminating your limiting beliefs, it's time to begin creating some new beliefs; ones that will support you and your desires.

Think about what you want in your life. What would someone need to believe in order to be living the type of life you desire? For example, wealthy people have no trouble believing they're wealthy, mainly because they are.

How does someone who is not wealthy, fit, successful, happy, or whatever it is they want to change, convince themselves that they are?

One of the best ways is to create an image of the person you want to become and devote some time each day to seeing yourself as this person. Similar to using affirmations, if one of your desires is to be financially wealthy, see yourself as this type of person. Feel the way you would feel if you have already achieved wealth. In your imagination, see yourself acting the way you would if you were already wealthy. How are you using your wealth?

The thing to understand that, in our fantasy, your subconscious mind does not distinguish between what is real and what is vividly imagined, with feeling.

It's important to note here that the feeling, the emotion you feel, is what is working to attract and manifest your desires.

As a man thinketh in his heart, so is he."
Proverbs 23:7

AFFIRM YOUR DESIRES

Any statement or thought, held in your mind and repeated over and over, with feeling, will over time, be accepted by and acted upon by our subconscious mind.

This is why when you repeatedly tell a child how you perceive them, they will begin to believe and act upon the statement. Tell the child they are loved, accepted, creative, and talented over and over and they will grow up believing and demonstrating this encouraging behavior.

Unfortunately, the opposite is also true. Tell them repeatedly they're not smart and will never get ahead and you will have, perhaps unintentionally, contributed to the creation of their limiting beliefs. This is why so many people in our society suffer from low self-esteem.

Something I learned as a volunteer, delivering my success seminars in our local prison over a twenty-year period, is that most of the people serving time (if not all of them) are suffering from a poor self-image and low self-esteem.

I believe that it is low self-esteem that is the root of many of the problems plaguing our present society. Alcoholics, drug addicts and, as I mentioned, most criminals have low self-esteem. One of the best ways to guide children away from drug addiction is to raise them to have a healthy self-image and high self-esteem. People with a strong sense of their own self-worth rarely resort to drugs, alcohol, gambling, etcetera. Since they already feel good about themselves, they have little reason to do these things. It is the person with low self-esteem that wants to change the way they feel emotionally and is more likely to turn to substances as a solution.

REPETITION IS KEY

The more you repeat and affirm your new beliefs, the faster and more strongly they will take hold. You can write them twenty-five to fifty times a day. You can sing or recite them throughout your day. You can write them on notes or signs and post them where you will see them regularly.

It is this constant repetition of our empowering affirmations that impresses them on our conscious mind, and which ultimately enables them to be accepted as truth by your subconscious.

Once a belief is accepted, your subconscious will guide you to see opportunities that were previously not visible to you. You will notice synchronicities happening in your experience. You may be guided to a particular book or website that will move you in the direction of your desires. Devoting time to vividly imagine being the person you want to be and living the life you desire will guide you to your successes in due time.

It is important to remember, changing your limiting beliefs is only the beginning. It is not enough by itself. Beliefs are dormant or unfulfilled potential. Just because I want to write a book and believe I can, does not mean it will be written and fall into my lap. It is your action that will manifest your desires.

DECISIONS

*"Between stimulus and response
there is a space. In that space lies
our freedom and power to choose
our response. In those choices lie
our growth and happiness."*
Viktor E. Frankl

*"It is in the moments of decision that
your destiny is shaped."*
Anthony Robbins

The process of decision making is arguably the most important of our cognitive activities. For the most part, it is the results of our individual and cumulative choices that shape our lives. But even a single decision can have a dramatic impact and send us in a direction that we could never have predicted.

Look back on your life for a moment. Can you identify any choices that you may have thought were small and inconsequential, but ultimately had a major impact on what happened later in life? Do you see missed opportunities because of bad decisions you made or your failure to make a decision at all? Do you experience wonderful outcomes because of a choice you made?

How might your life be different if you were more aware and intentional about your decisions? This is what we will explore.

In my personal life, I made a simple decision in the early days of my career to go on an interview for a job in an industry about which I was a bit curious and interested, but of which I knew very little. That decision started me on a path to an extremely successful, 35-year career in the mortgage industry. Of course, there were many other decisions (good and bad) that I made along the way which contributed to the results in my career, but it started with that seemingly small decision.

For my co-author, Jim Donovan, it was a small decision one day to write and share an article about some of the things he was learning as he reconstructed his life after battling addiction. That simple decision has led him to authoring nine books, and co-coauthoring several others, and led him to a life he could have only imagined.

To be able to make decisions that will help us create the change we want in our lives, we must be more intentional. We need to understand how our mind makes decisions and what prevents us from making decisions that support our goals. Then, we must determine how to make decisions that will produce those desired objectives.

The fact is, while we are awake, we are constantly making decisions. It has been estimated that we make approximately 35,000 decisions every day. Assuming we sleep for 8 hours, that would be almost 2,200 decisions per hour or 36 decisions each minute.

Most of these are small decisions that don't require much effort or brain power, such as getting a drink of water, selecting our lunch, or choosing a pair of socks.

Additionally, many of these low priority or low impact decisions are made subconsciously. In these situations, we are completely unaware that we are making a decision. For example, if you travel to a work location each day, many of the steps you take in driving or taking public transportation to your destination are a series of unconscious decisions. In fact, decisions like this actually develop into a habit. We will explore the subject of habits in greater detail in the next chapter.

These unconscious decisions can be near impossible to control, because we are essentially running on auto-pilot. They are choices we make from perceived options, which we subconsciously select. More often than not, these choices are based on feelings of comfort or familiarity, even if they are not always in our best interest.

At the other end of the decision spectrum are the impactful or extremely important decisions. Such as, "Are we really in the position to buy that house?" "Should I leave my secure job to jump into my own business?" "Has my relationship with my spouse reached the point where we need to seek counseling"?

Can you also see how these decision questions lead to other questions that could further complicate the issue and how they escalate the potential impact on our future? This continuous flow of questions and the decisions that follow are all part of our decision-making process.

The challenge to making our best decisions as we deal with these questions is, we don't actually understand the decision-making process. And, because of that and our busy lives, we don't give these types of questions the critical thinking time they deserve.

Most of us adults believe that we are rational thinkers and that the decision-making process is fairly simple and straight-forward. We think that we make sound decisions for ourselves. However, the decision-making process in the human mind is a bit more complex than we realize and our decisions are susceptible to internal struggles and laziness of our minds.

In his best-selling book, "Thinking, Fast and Slow", psychologist Daniel Kahneman, reveals a very different description of what goes on in our brains at decision time. In fact, his work on the psychology of judgement and decision-making challenges the assumptions of human rationality that have been part of modern economic thinking. It was for his work in this area for which he was awarded the Nobel Prize in Economic Science in 2002. But the implications of his discovery have far reaching effects in all aspects of human nature and our ability to understand ourselves and others.

The books core thesis is about the functioning and contrast between two modes of thinking that exist in our minds and how we use these to make our decisions:

System 1, is a fast, unconscious, intuitive, and emotional way of thinking. It operates with little or no effort and no sense of voluntary control. This mode of thinking has been with us since our earliest human existence and is vital to our survival. Assuming you are not walking and texting at the time, this is the system that makes you instantaneously jump out of the way of a car that honks its horn at you, a decision that is totally unconscious.

System 2 is slower, more conscious, deliberate, analytical and, logical. It requires problem solving, reasoning, concentrating, computing, considering alternate information, and to resist jumping to quick conclusions. It is best applied to complex activity and situations that require our focus and effort such as preparing our tax return, the evaluation of investment options, or determining how to handle a health problem. Also, it is with this thinking that we purposely guide our attention and exert self-control.

However, the problem is, at times there are unconscious internal struggles to determine which system will be in charge in certain decision situations. This battle of the systems over who's in charge can leave us susceptible to errors in judgement and poor decisions.

"Most of our judgments and actions are appropriate most of the time," says Kahneman. Yet what he discovered was "systematic errors in the thinking of normal people;" errors that came not just from emotion-based influences, but that had been incorporated into our cognitive processes.

According to Kahneman, the mind is basically lazy. And because of our mental laziness, it tends to take the easier course and not examine all available decision data. Instead, it uses shortcuts or "rules of thumb" to make it simpler and less demanding to make decisions, leaning heavily on System 1, thus, not using the full power of our intelligence.

Intelligence in this context refers not just to our ability to apply reason, but to our ability to tap into our memory to access relevant information and to direct our attention in appropriate situations.

The fact is, when we are faced with a difficult decision, it requires a great deal of mental and even physical energy to properly examine and analyze the problem and come up with the best solution. You will note that when someone is walking and they are asked to solve something complex like a difficult math problem, they usually stop to focus their time and energy on a solution.

But people don't realize that. We think that our decision making is under our control at all times. The truth is that when we are tired, hungry, mentally exhausted, or stressed, our self-control becomes weak. Instead of taking the time and effort to think through a problem as we should, we subconsciously look for the easy answer. This makes us prone to letting System 1 take over, making decisions intuitively and impulsively.

Kahneman also describes the cognitive biases related to each type of thinking and how they compound the struggle of both systems wanting to be in charge.

A Cognitive Bias is defined as, "a mistake in reasoning, evaluating, remembering, or other cognitive processes, often occurring as a result of holding onto one's preferences and beliefs regardless of contrary information." It might be a commonly held belief and may appear to be based in rational thought, but it is the cause of most of our bad decisions.

These cognitive biases become part of our intuition. As such, they can cause us to automatically make assumptions without giving thorough examination and analysis. Unfortunately, these cognitive illusions are not easily detected. And so, we make many of our decisions based on beliefs formed from what we've learned, have been told by a reliable source, or have experienced in our life, even though the belief may actually be false.

An interesting example of the results of bad decisions based on a bias would be the death of our first president, George Washington. Washington, at age 67, was in rather good health. However, a few days after a ride around his estate at Mt. Vernon on a wet, cold weather day in mid-December, he developed a sore throat and had trouble breathing.

A common belief in those days was that the extraction of some blood from an ill person would help heal them. So, it was Washington who asked his overseer to bleed him and call for his doctors. The doctors arrived and proceeded to take blood from him 4 more times in an 8-hour period. The result was a 40% loss of blood and an extremely compromised immune system. Washington died within 21 hours.

At that time in history, medicine was more art than science, nothing close to what we have today. The bias of doctors for bloodletting as a way to cure people was extremely strong. Of course, modern medicine has since advanced and shown this practice to actually be detrimental to the patient.

I think it is easy to see how a bias introduced into our normal decision-making process can move us in directions which don't support the results we are trying to achieve.

Here, let me bring the ego back into the discussion for a moment.

The ego has a huge influence on our thinking, particularly around the operation of "System 2" thinking, those occasions when we have impactful or complex decisions to make.

In situations where we use System 2, the ego will often draw on our cognitive biases about knowledge we've accumulated. It wants us to believe that we have all the information necessary, all the answers, to make the right decision.

This is particularly unfortunate, as we miss opportunities that could lead to exploration of different ideas that would stretch our thinking and enable us to see new possibilities and solutions.

This discussion of our decision-making processes was intended to help you form an understanding of the challenges we create with our thinking. Now that you're aware of the challenges, let's determine what we can do to take more control of this powerful tool in order to begin to create more of the change we want in our life.

Of all of the decisions we make in different parts of our lives, there are three types of decisions that will be a major determinant for the results we get:

Focus Decisions - The things we decide to focus our attention on

Meaning Decisions - The meaning we decide to give to things

Action Decisions - The actions we decide to take toward our goals

OUR FOCUS DECISIONS

If we aren't creating the change we want to see in our lives, we need to carefully examine our decisions. The first place we should look is at our choices regarding our focus. Lack of focus is one of the main reasons we don't achieve our goals.

This starts by understanding that the power to create any results in our lives is fueled by our expectation of what will happen. You may have heard the expression, "Expectation manifests into creation." This refers to the powerful conscious and subconscious energies that are released when we strongly hold an expectation, good or bad. This is true for events, material things, even our personal development.

But where does expectation come from? Actually, it is our thoughts that produce our expectations.

Earlier, I mentioned Earl Nightingale's definition of success from his recording "The Strangest Secret". This definition by itself is a pearl of wisdom. But the real life-changing gem he delivers in this classic is this message . . . "We become what we think about."

He goes on to quote the Bible and numerous great minds from history, who tell us that what we continually think about expands in our minds. Therefore, it is this expansion or development from our thinking that ultimately determines who and what we become. Through the ages, there have been a plethora of books that have shown us the association of our thinking to the results life gives us. "The Magic of Thinking Big", "As a Man Thinketh" and "Think and Grow Rich" are titles that immediately come to mind.

So, if we become what we think about, we had better be really careful about where our thoughts go.

This begs the question: what causes us to think about something in particular? Because, if we can understand this aspect, we would know how to direct and control the focus of our thoughts in a way that will help create the life we want.

It seems that most of us believe that we control (decide) what we think about. But, as we learned when we discussed the research of Daniel Kahneman, that is only true part of the time and most of our decisions are produced unconsciously.

Unless intentionally directed to a subject, our thoughts are mainly controlled by whatever input we allow to enter our mind, especially through the eyes and ears. And even when intentionally directed, staying focused is difficult to maintain, because our senses are under a constant barrage from external sources like the media, advertising and entertainment options from our electronic devices, all vying for our attention and often winning.

Remember, the mind operates like an incredible computer. Without judgement, it simply takes what it receives, stores it in memory and then uses that input and associated data to run the appropriate programs that direct our actions. So, as they say in the computer world, garbage in, garbage out.

This means that where our attention (focus) goes, our mental energy flows. And, since that is the direction of our mental energy, it determines our future. That is, what controls our focus, controls our life.

Since we know that our thoughts control the results we get in life, it is vital to guard what we put into our minds through our eyes and ears, as well as our intentional thinking. To successfully follow the "why" of our life, to attain specific goals, we must keep our focus on what we want, not a hundred other things that divert our attention and waste our most precious resource . . . time.

But, for most people, guarding the flow of input into our minds can be an extremely difficult task. Just think about those thousands of potential distractions coming into the brain through the eyes and ears each day (personal and work distractions, marketing messages, self-created distractions, etc.).

We may enjoy spending our time watching TV or our favorite online streaming programs, engaging on Facebook, LinkedIn and other social networks, playing video games, hanging out at the local bar, chatting with people on the phone, diddling with worthless emails, and the list goes on. But in our current world, involvement in these activities has become extreme for large portions of the population. In some cases, it can be categorized as an addiction. And for this, there is a price to pay.

Statistics show that the average American, eighteen years or older, watches about five hours of television each day. That's roughly 2,000 hours per year, which is the equivalent of seventy-two days out of the year. And this is just one area.

Do you see how allowing ourselves to focus on things like this eats up our time? It's not surprising to hear someone (or ourselves) say, "I just don't have enough time to get everything done." The truth is, that we lack the discipline to keep our focus on those things that align with our "why" and that can move us in the direction of the change we want?

I'm not saying we should never participate in and enjoy these things. My point is, that when our focus is unmanaged, these enjoyable activities can easily become unconscious actions that devour our precious time; time which could be focused on life changing options. Sadly, a majority of us are not even aware we are doing this to ourselves.

Another type of focus decision that undermines our ability to create change is our unconscious choices to focus on negative aspects associated with our goals or our ability to achieve those goals. If we choose to focus on the reasons why we can't do something or why something won't work, our mind will look for evidence to prove us right.

Don't think that I'm suggesting that we ignore any negative information associated with our goals. That would be foolish. I am, however, warning you of the dangers of a constant focus on negative information with a fear-driven, "glass half empty" attitude. It is that kind of thinking that kills so many very worthy goals in our world today. (Refer back to the section of the book regarding beliefs to gain a sense of the impact that focusing on the negative can have).

On the other hand, if we focus on why we can do something or why we should make the attempt or why it will work, the mind will search and find evidence to support that, as well.

Clearly, it takes the right focus, consistently applied, to achieve our goals. Shortly, we will look at how we can create and maintain that proper focus.

CONTROLLING OUR FOCUS

How then, do we take back control of our focus?

Awareness-Elimination-Refocus

First, create **Awareness** by identifying the areas you've allowed to steal your focus and devour your time (social media platforms, television, video games, mindless surfing the internet, email obsession, etc.). List the 3 that consume most of your time and the approximate number of hours you spend on them.

    _____ _____ Hours/ Week
    _____ _____ Hours/ Week
    _____ _____ Hours/ Week

What would happen if you applied those hours to working on the change you want to see (your goals)?

Commit to **Eliminate** these time/focus bandits from your life. (Make part of your action plan.)

Refocus by committing to use the new-found time on high priority goal activities. (Make part of your action plan.)

In attempting to regain control, be patient with yourself. After all, we may have been using these behaviors for a long time and to replace them with other more supportive ones will take work and consistency. This will not happen overnight. Having said that, you also must still be tough on yourself. Stay with it. We will give you an additional step for controlling your focus at the end of this chapter.

OUR MEANING DECISIONS

As with our focus decisions, the meaning we decide to give those things we experience, both physically and mentally, has a dramatic effect on what we think or do next. It can cause us to move forward, stop or retreat. Like a catalyst in a chain reaction, this assignment of meaning to what happens in our lives can become the spark for an ongoing series of thoughts, decisions and actions that determine the direction of our lives.

This type of decision is largely affected by existing information and existing thought patterns that operate like computer programs in our brains. These programs are based on: your beliefs, your values, references to past experiences, as well as, your emotional (feelings) and physical state.

It's important to note that there is an area of the brain called the amygdala, where emotional processing takes place. The main role of the amygdala is our survival and safety. Part of the mental programs I mentioned play a huge role in our decision analysis. It is also the force behind the Pain/Pleasure Principle, which is our uncon-scious drive to avoid pain and seek pleasure in our life.

It is this part of the brain that is responsible for the risk-adverse nature of humans. Because of it, when faced with situations that generate feelings of uncertainty and fear, our natural tendency is to be overly cautious or avoid them. Unfortunately, this response will often cause us to automatically eliminate options that would actually be beneficial for us, if we had investigated further.

When presented with information, the brain looks to see if the input is consistent with our beliefs and values, what we've experienced in the past, and if it will create emotional and/or physical instability or danger. It then determines what level of risk/comfort is associated to the input. From that, our minds assign a meaning which essentially gauges how good or bad this is for us.

If the input matches well with our mental program-ming and poses little or no danger (establishing a comfort level), the input will be given a meaning that is acceptable to us at some level and we can proceed to use it in some capacity. If on the other hand, the input doesn't match up when analyzed and there is a sense of danger communi-cated by the brain, the input will be given a meaning that this is unacceptable or bad for us.

This all happens unconsciously and in an instant. Of course, an assigned meaning isn't good or bad in absolute terms. The brain assigns varying degrees between totally acceptable and totally unacceptable.

This unconscious process is always operating in our interpersonal relationships. It's easy to see how the misin-terpretation of an event or exchange with another person could lead to a decision to give a negative meaning that is detrimental to the relationship.

The key point is that our human nature, past experiences, biases, and stored information influence the meaning we give to things. Accordingly, it is that meaning which determines how we feel and thus respond.

Regardless of the situation or the motive, it is our unconscious evaluation that controls the meaning we give to the things we are experiencing. So, how can we ensure that we assign supportive meaning to decisions related to our goals and objectives?

DECIDING TO GIVE BETTER MEANING

To apply better meaning to the occurrences in our life, we need to tap into some of the areas we covered in the first half of the book. One key is to increase our *Awareness.* By learning to raise our consciousness and become self-aware in those moments when important goal-related events are taking place, we can slow down the mind. This allows us to engage System 2 and have it take over the decision process.

We also need to set an intention in our mind that we will purposefully be seeking supportive meaning for our decisions and focus on consistently holding that intention in our mind.

Once we have accomplished these first two steps, it's time to *open our minds* to other options. As we do so, we must be on guard to prevent ourselves from pre-judging any possibilities just because they are outside our comfort zone or in opposition to our beliefs.

Next, we should examine those other possibilities by applying *Different Thinking;* asking ourselves questions that challenge our old mode of thinking, questions that make us see different perspectives which we may not agree with.

Performing these steps while at the same time focusing on the achievement of our objective, puts us in a position to make positive, supportive decisions about the meaning of any goal-related situation we face.

We suggest going back to the earlier chapters that cover Self-Awareness and Thinking Differently to review the action steps for these areas.

Just realize, it will take practice to develop these tactics into habits. But, the effort will pay dividends.

OUR ACTION DECISIONS

When it comes to achieving the goals and objectives that help us create the change we want to see in our lives, the results we desire are ultimately determined by our decisions to take action and which actions we will take.

However, it should be obvious from the previous material covered that our ability to make good action decisions comes from being in control of our focus and meaning decisions. Mastering these decision areas is essential to enabling us to make good action choices. But, it doesn't guarantee that we will do so. There is another factor that will also influence our action decisions.

As we anticipate taking the steps to create change in our life, we look for a sense of certainty about what we will do and the outcome we will achieve from it. Unfortunately, whenever change is involved, we frequently have to deal in our mind with a sense of uncertainty.

Even though we have applied the right focus and developed supportive meanings, nagging subconscious questions like: "Am I ready for this?" "Where do I start?"

"What if I fail?" can creep into our thinking. This causes stress. And when we are under stress about what to do, how to do it, or the likelihood of success, we are prone to postpone taking action, because as humans, we want certainty in our life.

As we unpack this issue of uncertainty, we realize that it is actually driven by fear. Fear of looking bad. Fear of failure. Fear of success. It comes in many forms which can undermine our best intentions to take action.

Let's face it. Change can be scary. When we attempt to do things in a different way or certainly, an action we've never done before, it is natural to experience some level of fear.

The logical question becomes, what can we do to overcome the fear we may have and create more certainty so that we can begin making decisions to take action?

First of all, it is important to understand that uncertainty is part of life. We can strive for certainty all we want, but to insist on it is just crazy. There are too many factors outside of our control to have total certainty. So, the best thing to do is to make friends with it. Learn to embrace it. Start looking for the opportunities hidden within uncertainty. Author Eckhart Tolle said, "When you become comfortable with uncertainty, Infinite Possibilities open up in your life."

It is also helpful to realize that the main reason for our feelings of doubt and fear come from a lack of self-confidence. Self-confidence is a feeling of trust or faith in our abilities.

When it comes to making action decisions, it is not just our knowledge and capability in a particular goal area that gives us confidence, but also the specific ability to consistently make decisions and then execute on them, even in the face of uncertainty.

It's a bit of a chicken and egg situation. The more we practice making decisions and executing, the more we build our self-confidence. The stronger our self-confidence, the greater our ability to make decisions and take action.

Here are some things you can do to develop your self-confidence:

Find Your Experience - Look into your past to see where you've taken action in uncertain situations and/or where you've successfully experienced something similar to what you are facing. It does not need to be exactly the same, just similar enough to show your past ability to handle uncertainty.

Plan and Prepare - Review what it is you want to accomplish. Evaluate the action you are considering to determine what options are available. Then, look at the pros and cons of each option. Selecting the best option, construct a plan for the steps you need to take to make it happen.

Then, determine what resources you will need. Be sure to do this in writing, not in your head. Having clear "next steps" will begin to create certainty. Recall the old saying; "Pre-planning prevents poor performance."

Visualize - In your mind, see yourself successfully taking each step of your plan and achieving the final outcome you want to experience. Repeat this each day as you move through your plan.

The more we focus on our similar past successes, plan and prepare, and visualize the execution and outcomes we want, the greater our confidence grows. As it does, the more likely we are to make those action decisions even with uncertainty surrounding them.

Keep in mind that many of your decisions will not yield the result you want. It is important to allow ourselves to fail. Each time we don't get the result we intended, we have to see these as experience, steps in our learning process. From such vantage points, we can use those lessons to make course corrections as we move closer to realizing the change we want in our life.

This possibility of failure brings us back to an area we touched on previously which is a factor that can affect our ability to make action decisions:

Commit - The act of making a firm commitment is a test to determine if we are adamant about achieving the objective we've set for ourselves. If we are not willing to persevere when we stumble and fall, if we are not willing to pick ourselves back up and continue to press forward, we have to ask how much we really want what we say we want.

If we have worked to define our *purpose*, our *"why"* and have set goals that are in alignment with them, it is much easier to make decisions to take action regardless of the challenges and uncertainty.

We want to suggest that you revisit your *purpose* and your *Why* to solidify your commitment. It is total commitment that empowers you to take action.

HABITS

*"Our character is basically a
composite of our habits. Because they
are consistent, often unconscious
patterns, they constantly, daily,
express our character."*
Stephen Covey

*"The chains of habit are too
weak to be felt until they are
too strong to be broken."*
Samuel Johnson

Even though we may have the right beliefs and are making conscious decisions that support the achievement of our goals, there is one additional piece of the puzzle which will be a significant determinant of the end result. Our habits.

We have mentioned it in a few places within the book. But now, we are going to get into the nuts and bolt of it and why it is so important.

We are all creatures of habit. There is no escaping that fact. But to use this to our advantage, we need to be asking ourselves questions, such as: How well are our current habits serving us? What thoughts and actions need to become habits in order to help us achieve our goals? How do we do that?

Habits are the formation of automatically performed routines, rituals or behaviors that enable us to do things more easily and with less effort. They are very closely associated with the Fast Thought System (System 1) we talked about earlier. You might think of them as a product of the Fast Thought System, in that, our mind uses a series of decisions generated by the Fast Thought System to create what would be similar to computer software programs that become wired into our brain and automatically executes when a certain stimulus triggers the program.

They are developed in our brains as a way to make its job easier, conserving energy (less processing effort) and reducing stress. In fact, if we didn't have habits to handle much of our daily activities, our days would be consumed by the constant processing of simple daily activities. Furthermore, we would be left mentally and physically exhausted.

Therefore, the more habits that the brain can create, the more energy and effort it has to apply to more complex activities and thinking (System 2).

A study at Duke University has shown that between 40 and 45% of what we think and do during our day is not determined by our decisions, but by our habits. So, it's easy to see the critical function they perform in our lives. But people are generally unaware that most of these habits exist or that they could be creating dysfunction and subverting the achievement of our goals.

A good example of this is your personal computer or mobile devices. As mentioned in the chapter on Decisions and Choices, they've had a huge positive impact on how we live our lives. However, certain aspects of their use have become bad habits and in extreme cases addictions. People don't notice how frequently they check email and social media, or the amount of time they spend playing computer gaming, watching videos of cats or kids and general web surfing. These activities have become habits which negatively alter their behavior and consume large portions of their time that could be used in more important aspects of their lives, like achieving goals they've set.

Undoubtedly, we will meet with many obstacles and challenges like this that affect our ability to take the right actions required for our success. To handle this, we need to recognize the habits we have and make the appropriate modifications to ensure we are consistently moving toward our objectives.

In this chapter, we will explore what habits are, how they can aid or inhibit us as we attempt to reach higher levels of success, and what we need to do to eliminate non-supportive habits or form supportive ones.

"Depending on what they are, our
habits
will either make or break us.
We become what we repeatedly do"
Sean Covey

Researchers have found that there is a three-part process that the brain goes through in forming a habit. It is referred to as the Habit Loop.

First, there is a cue which acts as a signal for the brain to go into automatic mode and decide which of its stored activity patterns to use.

Next is the routine. These are the activity patterns we've created for ourselves. It is possible for the routine to be physical, mental or emotional. And, as mentioned, they may serve us in a positive or negative way.

The last part of the process is the reward. It is the value of the reward which the brain uses to decide if it wants to remember a loop. The rewards can also be physical, mental or emotional.

As a loop is repeated over and over, the neural connections associated with the cue, routine and reward strengthen and they become a habit. Then, as it continues, the habit can become automatic to the point where it is totally unconscious.

As stated previously, our brains are basically lazy and are always looking to save energy. It will, in fact, attempt to make any routine into a habit.

Since habits do play such a big role in the actions we take, you can imagine how they become a determinant in the results we produce in our lives.

Another interesting and important aspect of the research was that the cue and the reward may become so connected with each other that an extremely strong anticipation can be triggered as soon a cue is introduced. This anticipation is what we commonly refer to as a *craving*. This craving is the real power that drives a habit.

It's interesting to note that companies have very successfully used this concept in their products and advertising to motivate people to purchase or continue to make purchases anytime the cue is presented.

Once a habit is formed, the brain begins to discontinue participating in the decision-making process associated with that activity or task. The more ingrained the habit is, the less thought the brain will direct to the activity until it finally stops altogether. At this point, it allows this automatic mechanism (the habit loop) to take over so the brain can focus on other situations and tasks. It's easy to see why addictions can be held in place so strongly once the habit is formed.

Also, those habits (programs) are always held in the brain ready for recall. They do not disappear. This is great for useful or productive habits. It means we don't have to relearn activities we've previously mastered if they have not been used for a period of time.

Last year, I experienced this personally when I was invited to go skiing for the first time in twenty-four years. With a little concern in the back of my mind, I left the ski lodge for the slopes. But what I found as I made my initial run was that the skiing techniques I had learned returned to me rather quickly. These habits were installed in me long ago and were retained for twenty-four years!

But since the brain doesn't distinguish between good and bad habits, the same is true for the bad ones. It merely executes routines on the appropriate cue. Therefore, bad habits cannot be eliminated. They can only be replaced with a better habit. That is what becomes the challenge, because replacing a habit can be extremely difficult as many smokers have discovered.

Difficult or not, there is evidence that a habit can be controlled, changed or replaced. The success of the twelve-step processes used by Alcoholics Anonymous for overcoming addiction is excellent proof. But as we've noted, once formed, the habit is still in the brain available to be triggered. That's why recovering addicts know they are just one drink or one fix from being drawn back into their problem.

So, regarding achieving success, there are habits that will support achievement and habits that will obstruct it. Unfortunately, the majority of people struggle with habits that don't support success. Because of our human drive to create or increase pleasure, we are attracted to activities that deliver some type of gratification and are easily formed into habits. Activities like video games, watching television, social media, internet surfing, and shopping can turn into time consuming habits. If unrestricted, the participation in these will expand, continuing to consume productive time that could be applied to goal oriented activities.

Take for example the young boy, who we'll call Tommy. He received a tablet computer at an early age and discovered the fun of playing video games. As he got older, and without limitations enforced by his parents, the amount of time he spent playing video games continued to increase.

He also started playing baseball for a youth team in his area with his friends from school. As with any sport, musical instrument or extracurricular activity, baseball requires a commitment of time to the development of skills in order to improve proficiency and to enable a person to better enjoy that activity. Actually, he was already doing that with the video games.

Since Tommy gave every spare minute he had to playing video games, he rarely invested time into improving his baseball skills. As his friends' skills advanced, Tommy's failed to develop. He eventually became discouraged by his lack of progress and quit playing baseball. Not surprisingly, he also saw his grades continue to slip. The habit was taking its toll on his life.

This could have easily been a story about a grown man named Tom, who now in his forties, has recently become aware of his health and physical appearance as well as his stagnant career. The problem is that he has developed habits around his favorite activities; watching television or online programming and drinking beer every day after work to the point where he is overweight, in terrible physical condition and unmotivated.

Last year, he joined a gym, but stopped going after 2 months. His career advancement went much the same way. He took one college course in his field before reverting back to the comfort of his TV and computer habits. Unfortunately, this description or some variation of it, depicts a large segment of the adult population.

So, you see, habits are a two-edged sword. The key to success is knowing which edge you are using.

In his book, *The Power of Habit,* Charles Duhigg (Random House, 2014) writes:

> *"Habits are powerful, but delicate. They can emerge outside our consciousness, or can be deliberately designed. They often occur without our permission but can be reshaped by fiddling with their parts. They shape our lives far more than we realize. They are so strong, in fact, that they cause our brains to cling to them at the exclusion of all else, including common sense."*

Another issue is that we are typically not aware of these habit loops as they begin to form and develop. Therefore, in the case of bad habits, they may start gradually and inconspicuously until we discover that we are dealing with a super strong habit. At that point, changing the habit becomes a serious challenge.

The good news is that by learning how habits loops work, people can begin to control their lives through the manipulation of bad habits and the creation of new ones. This is what is referred to as habit replacement.

The key to habit replacement is to use the same cue and reward from the bad habit loop but replace the problematic behavior/routine with a positive routine that supports the change we want. That is, if we can alter or replace the routine which is triggered by that familiar cue and maintain a sufficiently strong reward, we have the basis for affecting positive change in our life.

Think of someone who wants to reduce an out of control TV or computer viewing habit. Perhaps, when they finish eating dinner (the cue), they usually go to their TV, computer or mobile device and begin to indulge in an evening of mindless viewing and surfing (the routine). Their mind enjoys the pleasure of beings entertained (the reward).

A replacement routine to form their new habit could be to go for a walk after dinner while listening to a good audio book. They may attach a note to any screens or devices that reminds them to go for a walk instead of watching. They could also place their sneakers there to provide reinforcement.

ACTIVITY STEP

In order to create the change needed to replace the habits that don't support our success, we must start with awareness and reflection. This means identifying what we want, what's blocking us and determining what actions will move us toward our goal.

Complete the following questions and directives:

- What is the goal or objective I'm focusing on?
- Which habits (behaviors) do I have that are obstacles to achieving that goal? (Note: some

activities may not appear to be related to your goal, but are still an obstacle to it.)
- What is the cue, the routine and the reward associated with each habit?

Since it is the current routine (action) related to a particular cue that is blocking my progress,

- What new routine(s) should be substituted into the habit loop which would move me toward my goal? (Define the specific actions)
- How can I enhance the reward to make it more powerful?
- What additional reinforcement can I use to ensure the formation of this habit?
- Write out the new habit (cue, new routine and reward) as a statement. For example: "Every day after dinner, I walk 3 miles while listening to an audio book. I get tremendous pleasure from hearing fascinating stories or educational information while improving my health".
- Review your beliefs to ensure they support your new habits.
- Each morning, write your new habit statement.
- Describe what resistance you may encounter and how you'll handle it.

Keep in mind, if you are forming an entirely new habit, you will need to create a cue and a reward to associate with the action you have chosen.

Note here that the old cue and reward are very important to the habit replacement, but by themselves, are not enough to have a new habit continue. We have to get our brain to start anticipating the reward. There needs to be a craving for the reward or a strong motivation that drives us to repeat the action. From this, a new habit will be formed.

So, the more we can relate the reward to our goal and especially our personal "why," the greater leverage we can use on ourselves to perform the desired action and to continue it.

Also, by writing down our new routine and keeping it visible to us throughout the day, we maintain our brain's conscious focus on creating the new habit. You can use this and other goal creation techniques in the same way.

JASON'S STORY

Jason was a commissioned loan officer for a regional mortgage banking company. He had recently started his career in the mortgage industry. Married with two young children, his big goal was to create a consistent commission flow that would enable he and his wife to buy their first home.

But, Jason was struggling to generate enough income to pay his monthly bills let alone save the needed money and afford a mortgage payment for a home. In fact, he was beginning to fear that he would be fired for lack of production.

As we examined his habits, we found that he was spending a disproportionate amount of time on his mobile phone or laptop, checking email, text messages or social media. *(the routine).* This unfocused activity led him down the internet rabbit hole and into hours of unproductive time during his day. It also was a constant disruption to high priority activities that would lead to success.

In this case, one of *the* cues that triggered his pro-ductivity-killing habit was the sound of the notifications from his mobile phone or laptop.

The *reward* was the feeling of satisfaction he got from being busy and, in his mind, giving good service by responding immediately to any and all notifications. He was getting a mental rush whenever he heard the notifi-cations and took action, especially when someone liked or commented on one of his social media posts.

After identifying the cue, routine and reward, we began to look for a new routine to substitute for the old problem routine. As we helped him evaluate new habit possibilities, he chose three marketing- lead generation activities that he wanted to do consistently each day.

Then, he turned off the automatic email, text and social media sound notifications and set an alarm on his mobile phone and laptop, which would go off at three specific times throughout the day (the cue). When the alarms sounded, he would spend the next hour without interruption executing the scheduled marketing or lead generation activities (the new routine). The reward for the activities was the satisfaction of productivity and knowing he was moving a step closer to his goal (their first home) each day.

To ensure the strength of the reward, he found a picture of a home similar to what he wanted and pho-to-shopped a picture of his family into it (his goal and his "why"). He placed this as the background of the home screen of his laptop and his mobile phone. To increase his focus, each morning he would write out the new habit he wanted to form.

Gradually, when the alarms went off, Jason would think about their new home and the feeling of satisfaction from being truly productive. This became the new craving that drove his new habit (this and a little encouragement from his wife as well).

After setting this habit in place, he used this successful habit as inspiration to start forming other good productivity habits.

Just over nine months after he created his first new habit, Jason became one of the top ten loan originators in his company. With the increase in income, he and his wife were able to buy their first home.

CHANGING HABITS WITH THE POWER OF BELIEF

Research has shown that there are two other critical aspects that foster habit replacement. The first is the power of belief, which we covered earlier in this book. A person looking to create change in a habit must hold a deep faith that the habit and the related circumstances can be changed and will improve.

This belief factor is evident in the 12-step of Alcoholics Anonymous which is one of the most successful habit change processes ever discovered.

With strongly ingrained bad habits, it can be extremely difficult to change and thus the greater the possibility that the new habit can fail, causing the person to fall back into the old habit. Remember, the old habit is always there, ready to resurface.

It's interesting to note that research interviews with alcoholics indicated that while changing the elements of the habit loop were important to their success, they said the key factor in sustained sobriety was God.

Evidence has shown that an association of a Higher Power to the beliefs of the alcoholic about being able to change the habit was what sustained their ability to stay sober when others who did not have such strong beliefs were highly susceptible to resume drinking with the next stressful life event.

A strong belief that the challenge can be overcome, that the new habit can work, and that you will change, is needed to get through difficult times. As mentioned in the earlier discussion of beliefs, you are empowered or disempowered by the beliefs you cultivate and maintain.

It is advisable to go back to the chapter on beliefs to review the tips on forming empowering beliefs relative to forming new habits.

LEVERAGING THE POWER OF COMMUNITY

The other element vital to habit replacement is community. If a person joins a group or aligns with even one other person who contributes to their belief that change is possible for them and provides opportunities to talk through the challenges to change that will surely arise, the likelihood of the new habit continuing increases dramatically.

People who cling exclusively to their own thinking can be doubtful about their ability to change. However, there is a power that is generated through the shared experiences of a group. This power helps them suspend their doubts, begin to build their belief and continually confirm it as it grows.

Once again, Alcoholics Anonymous provides a wonderful example of the effectiveness of community through the AA group members and their sponsor, who teach the alcoholic to believe they can stay sober and help sustain that belief.

Another example is Weight Watchers, the international weight loss organization, which uses community to provide information, accountability, motivation and inspiration to its members.

This community effect concept of habit creation is one of the factors on which one-on-one coaching, group coaching and mastermind groups have been established and a reason for their effectiveness. As with the sobriety and weight loss organizations mention above, these developmental processes help maintain the focus on our target goals, the habit change we need to reach them and the beliefs that both of these are possible.

But there are additional aspects of the community effect concept that need to be present for it to truly work. First, we must be committed to active involvement and consistent in our participation in our mastermind or coaching program. By doing so, it facilitates the creation of a new habit that becomes a springboard for the creation of other habits. This is referred to as a Keystone Habit. As we saw in Jason's story, the cumulative effect of supportive habits is what leads us to the ultimate change we want to see.

Of course, there are those who will choose to attempt it on their own, relying on self-discipline and personal accountability to form or replace habits. The reality is, the large majority of people don't have the sustained discipline to do this on their own. The existence and growth of the many organizations and programs that utilize the community effect concepts is further evidence of this.

When we become part of a mastermind group or coaching program, we are joining forces with one or more people who can keep us accountable and celebrate our progress. Making a commitment to our coach or group members adds a positive pressure most people find difficult to create on their own.

To further help us keep that commitment, we should look to our "why" and ask ourselves questions.

Why do we want to form this habit?

How does it help us create the change we want to see?

What will happen if we continue doing what we've been doing?

We can't stress enough the value of the community effect concept. If you are serious about forming the habits and creating the change you want to see in your life, you should definitely explore investing in yourself by engaging with a good group coaching programs or mastermind groups, and one-on-one coaching programs.

If we are to redesign our habits to better support the big, life impact goals we want, we have to apply all of the change agents previously covered: *open mindedness, awareness, taking responsibility, thinking differently* and *making a commitment.* Refer back to these areas of the book for review.

One final thought about habits. Our willpower, our self-discipline, is like a muscle. Once we start practicing the habit, focusing on the reward and repeat it regularly, our willpower muscle will get stronger and stronger. Studies show that the more we develop this "muscle", we will find it easier to form other positive habits.

So, when will you start forming the habits that create the change you want to see? What action will you take? Perhaps you should join a mastermind group, a group coaching program or hire a coach to give you the guidance, focus, and accountability you need to ensure results.

You already know that being an action taker is one of the primary keys to success in anything. Take action by doing the earlier exercise. Get started on forming this habit, right now.

> *"The law of harvest is to reap*
> *more than you sow. Sow an act,*
> *and you reap a habit. Sow a habit*
> *and you reap a character. Sow a*
> *character and you reap a destiny."*
>
> James Allen

BRIAN PROPP'S STORY

There are times in our lives when we are forced to face change; the kind that turns our entire world upside down and inside out. Some people refer to this change as a tragedy. I prefer to call them extreme challenges. Unexpected and unwanted, they test our resolve to see how desperately we want something. They make us stronger. Let me tell you about a man who had to create change against incredible odds.

I have a friend in the Philadelphia area named Bran Propp. Brian is a retired professional ice hockey player who enjoyed fifteen seasons in the NHL from 1979 until 1994. A native of Saskatchewan, Canada, he was drafted fourteenth overall in 1997 NHL Entry Draft by the Philadelphia Flyers. During his rookie season, he played on a line with legends Reggie Leach and Bobbie Clarke.

In 1987, he was selected to the Canadian team that won the Canada Cup World Championship, where he was teamed with super stars, Wayne Gretzky and Mario Lemieux.

During his fifteen seasons in the NHL. Brian made it to the Stanley Cup Finals five times and played in five NHL All-Star game five times.

When he retired at the end of the 1994 season, he had amassed 1,004 points for his career. In Flyers history, only Bill Barber has scored more goals and Brian is third in assists behind Bobby Clarke and Claude Giroux. Quite an impressive list of achievements.

Despite being a grizzled veteran of a very tough sport, Brian is a very humble and caring guy. In talking about his success, he always defers to his coaches and teammates as part of the reason for his success.

But there were a few other ingredients in his success: his belief in himself, his coaches and teammates, the decisions he made throughout his career, and the habits he formed along the way.

Even after retirement from the professional game, he remained an incredible athlete, stayed in great shape, and played hockey with friends twice a week.

But of all the challenges and change he dealt with during his career, nothing compared to what he would face in retirement.

In 2002, Brian was diagnosed with Atrial Fibrillation or AFib, which is the most common type of irregular heartbeat. The abnormal firing of electrical impulses causes the atria (the top chambers in the heart) to quiver (or fibrillate). He had been under a doctor's care to manage this condition that afflicts many people. Brian had things under control.

However, in 2016, while preparing for a family vacation to Annapolis, MD, he noticed that he was not feeling well, but didn't want to ruin their plans. They left for vacation, while the feeling persisted.

Then, one night in his sleep he became extremely ill. In an attempt to get up, he fell out of bed, knocking out several teeth from the impact. Lying on the floor partially conscious, he realized that his right side was completely paralyzed, and he could not speak. He had suffered a stroke. EMTs rushed him to the hospital where they discovered that a huge blood clot had formed, broke off and went to his brain.

Here was this very successful former professional athlete, who had everything to live for, now facing the biggest challenge of his life.

For many people, this occurrence becomes an insurmountable obstacle. The beginning of the end. They essentially accept this as their fate.

But not for "Propper," as friends call him. He had the **belief** that he could overcome this huge physical and mental challenge that he faced. But belief was only his first step. He had made the **decision** to take control of his thinking and committed to do whatever was necessary to regain control of his life, to take every action he could.

Just as he pushed himself through his professional hockey career, developing his skills, and becoming a star, along the way, he **committed** himself to regaining a normal life.

The next two years were a schedule of continuous medical appointments: occupational therapy, physical therapy, speech therapy, even stem cell treatment. But just as he had done as a professional athlete, he formed the **habits** of thought and action that would ensure he did whatever the medical plan called for and more.

Since that fateful date, because of his **beliefs, decisions and habits**, Brian has regained control of his right arm and leg. He is back to skating again and has even recovered his speech.

In fact, Brian Propp now has a busy schedule speaking to groups about his story and relating to them **the power of their beliefs, decisions and habits to create the change they want to see in their lives.**

WHAT ARE YOU WAITING FOR?

*"Your life does not get better by chance.
It gets better by change."*
Jim Rohn

If you made it through to this chapter, congratulations! A significant percentage of readers don't finish the books they start, but you did. Now, what are you going to do?

One of Jim Donovan's early books is titled, *"What are you waiting for? It's Your Life,"* (Sound Wisdom, 2014). His message was to stop stalling, procrastinating, avoiding and waiting for the right time to make the changes in your life which have been on your mind for so long. Time is passing. And we only have one life to live. Wouldn't be a shame to be facing your final days here on earth and be haunted by the regret that you never found the courage and determination to answer that calling from deep within, to achieve your real potential.

We are put on this earth by a Creator who wants us to cherish, enjoy and share all aspects of life: the marvels of our physical being, the beauty of nature, the warmth of our relationships, the amazing abundance and wealth that is available to us. Also, He wants us to become all that we can be.

However, it seems to me that our ability to truly appreciate these things requires a frame of reference. That reference comes from our effort to explore and discover why we were put on this earth and then to pour ourselves into whatever we discover. It is going through the phases of this process that provides this sense of personal fulfillment. And, with that feeling, we are able to more fully enjoy all the other aspects of life, instead of pursuing them in hopes of finding fulfillment there.

Is there a risk of making the effort and possibly failing to create what we want? Absolutely, and that is certainly one of the reasons which holds many people back from achieving more. But the alternative of living a life that lacks inspiration and fulfillment is a sad waste of the God-given potential. Besides, even in a failed effort to achieve, we stretch ourselves beyond our abilities, learn, and as a result we grow, and as a result become a different person.

While the majority of people don't realize it, our lives have the potential to yield great abundance. Those people accept the limited thinking they have developed over the years. Yet, there is so much more that they can have if they were aware of that available abundance, knew how to tap into it and had the confidence to do so.

This abundance is within our reach if we can only develop *the right beliefs*, make *the right decisions*, and form *the right habits* that enable us to create what we desire. Whether we want a better education or job, improved health, a more loving relationship, a better life for our family, a successful business, or some hugely audacious goal that could change the lives of other people, it's all waiting for us to create it.

We have provided powerful information in this book. But, nothing will happen unless you put this knowledge into action. Yes, it will take real effort to manifest the things you want in life.

The good news is that when you do apply what you've learned here, it gets much easier to create the change you want. That's because as you diligently employ the ideas we've shared, you will change how you think and act, which has been the underlying objective of this book.

The newly developing "you" will be able to access your potential by getting clear on your vision, working to remove the roadblocks, remaining focused on your objectives and taking consistent action.

People have asked if someone can benefit by just working on one or two elements from the book. The answer is: yes. Each concept that we presented has the ability to improve the person who takes action on it. Being more aware, thinking differently and taking ownership will all help us. But keep in mind, to create the real change we want to see, we have to play full out in all of the key areas we covered, otherwise we may be limiting our own progress.

For example, if you replace the limiting beliefs that have been holding you back from achieving your goals, but continue to live with certain habits that undermine them, your struggles will persist.

On the other hand, when you focus on employing all elements, they work together in a synergistic manner to bring about the manifestation of what you truly want.

Our desire was to produce a book that gave you the knowledge, inspiration and practical guidance that can help you *Create the Change You Want to See in Your Life*. We sincerely hope we did that and hope that you completed the Action Steps we placed along the way. If you haven't, please go back and do them. These exercises were intended to give you a jump-start for the process of creating change. You see, having this knowledge is important, but it will be of little value unless you put it into use.

OBSTACLES ALONG THE WAY

Now, as we said, you will have to consistently work at this. It won't happen overnight. Even as you give your best efforts to bring about the change you want, you will certainly be challenged to overcome obstacles and distractions that you encounter along the way.

The stories of Vince Papale, Brian Propp, and Sequoras Johnson are three examples of the hard work and resilience needed to handle those stumbling blocks and setbacks.

To prepare you, here are a few of the obstacles and areas of resistance you may encounter:

Staying in your comfort zone - It's important to enjoy what we've already accomplished in life. But the fact is, many people strive until they find a comfortable existence and then begin to coast. They say they want to be, do, and have more, but rarely pursue it. They set up residence in their comfort zone. How about you? Are you satisfied staying in your comfort zone?

Lack of consistent effort - Unfortunately, consistent effort seems to be in short supply in our world. People give up way too soon when they encounter resistance, problems, distractions and challenges. Or they become bored and move on to the next shiny object life shows them. Will you have the discipline to continuously apply what you've learned?

Inability to see the limiting beliefs - There are blind spots in our belief system which must be replaced with empowering beliefs in order to achieve the results we want. But it's impossible to work on something you don't recognize. Will you be able to objectively see and change disempowering beliefs you have?

Inability or unwillingness to recognize the bad decisions - When we've made poor choices in regard to: what we are focused on, the meaning we give things or the actions we've taken, our ego tends to defend our decisions at the expense of our growth. Are you able to summon the necessary awareness and self-responsibility that enables you to push aside your ego and objectively call yourself out?

Being trapped in bad habits - Just like an addict who doesn't see the habits that have him trapped in his addiction, so it can be for all of us by not seeing habits that keep us from what we want. We may make some progress, but inevitably slip back into the bad habits that block our dreams. Can you be honest, objective and determined enough to be able to see and replace the bad habits or create new ones that support your goals?

> *"A good portion of the things you want*
> *in life is outside your comfort zone."*
> Idowu Koyenikan

SEQUORA'S STORY CONTINUED

As you will recall, earlier in this book, we began the story about a young woman named Sequora Johnston. Her life was spiraling painfully downward because of an eating disorder and consequential weight problem. While recovering from yet another injury, her weight had now escalated to 240 pounds. Feeling depressed and out of control, her self-esteem was at an all-time low.

Emotional states like this usually gave her the excuse to have a prolonged pity party. These unconscious **decisions** kept her trapped in a downward spiral.

But one day, as she was lying in bed with her swollen, purple, black and blue sprained ankle propped up and a heating pad on her back, a certain **awareness** came over her. As if a switch were triggered in her mind, a new level of consciousness enabled her to see the truth of her situation.

She related the thoughts of her epiphany. "I felt uncomfortable and unhealthy. I didn't like myself. I was not being the athlete and person I know I could be. Then, I realized it's not really a physical problem. It was not because of the bad things happening to me. The biggest part of my problem was mental. It was time to stop letting myself use these injuries and misfortunes as an excuse to eat more. There was no reason why I allowed my weight to get to this point. I knew I had to be responsible for myself and take control of what I was consuming and my physical health. I **decided** that if I have control over anything in my life, it's what I'm doing to my body."

This was a huge breakthrough. She began to **think differently** and **take action.**

As she was convalescing, Sequora took the opportunity to study the nutritional aspects of a healthy life style. She started **writing out her intentions** for **what she wanted to change** about herself. As she gained more knowledge, she started forming **habits** such as, writing out meal plans to follow as well as tracking her consumption and weight loss progress. Using delayed gratification, she found greater satisfaction which made her more motivated and determined.

This was also the point when she discovered the practice of yoga and yoga philosophy, which was a huge factor in her transformation. "Yoga changed my life," Sequora declared. "I don't think I would have ever lost the weight if it weren't for yoga."

From this ancient discipline, she learned to **be more conscious of her thoughts**, a vital concept she needed to form a foundation for change. Her daily yoga routine quickly became her **keystone habit.**

This **action decision** to use yoga and behavior modification to improve herself and lose weight, enabled her to be more consistently **conscious** of her **focus and meaning decisions.** As a result, she began making more decisions that supported her goal to create the change she wanted in her life.

Another **awareness** that emerged was of her **limiting beliefs** like, "it's okay for goal keepers or powerlifters to be overweight." These thoughts had been disempowering her and preventing her from addressing her weight issue.

Her new belief was that she could control what she put into her body and the actions necessary to be in good physical condition. This became a strong supporting belief **(habit of thought)** for her. The reward she derived was not just losing weight, but the great feeling of being in control of her thoughts and actions.

The journey wasn't linear or easy. Some days were much more challenging for losing weight. It was an ongoing battle. But she continued to strengthen her **beliefs**, make good **decisions** and work on her supportive **habits**. As a result, Sequora dropped her weight from 240 pounds to 155 pounds. That's an eighty-five pound difference! Talk about **Creating the Change You Want to See!**

An important lesson she learned was about the mind-body connection. It became apparent to her that the mind cannot be clear and operate effectively when the body is not receiving the proper nutrients it needs. Her interest in healthy and nutrition began to grow.

Through the process of her experience, lessons and growth, she discovered her *"Why"*. Sequora knew how hard the journey was. So, she **decide**d to dedicate herself to helping others, who were experiencing the pain, embarrassment and low self-esteem she went through. After finishing high school, she enrolled in college to become a Dietitian. As of the publication of this book, she has been receiving straight A's.

Living completely on her own, she works full-time to pay for her tuition, apartment rent and the car she purchased. And, by the way, she's still practicing her yoga **habit** every day.

It is amazing to meet a young person her age with the level of consciousness she has developed. The list of issues and challenges she dealt with in order to create the changes she wanted was mind-boggling: the sports injuries, poor self-image, the cyber school adjustment, full-time employment, while overcoming a severe eating disorder and weight problem.

If that wasn't enough, we later learned that during this period of struggle and growth, she was also helping her mother by paying a major portion of the mortgage on their home.

The maturity and self-awareness of this young woman, blew us away. She told us that the experiences she had, both good and bad, created the person she has become. "There's something to learn in everything," she said. "You just have to be open-minded to what is possible and **take responsibility for yourself."**

And, let me add to her wisdom; **think differently,** create **empowering beliefs,** make **conscious decisions** and form **habits that support** what you want to create in your life.

COMMITMENT AND THE NEXT STEP

To utilize the information in this book and work through the obstacles and areas of resistance, it will take a real commitment. Without a commitment to use what we've learned, we will likely continue to operate our lives with the same limiting beliefs, making the same poor decisions and accepting habits that block our progress.

It can be challenging and discouraging to work on these issues on our own. We strongly recommend that the reader consider the use of private or group coaching, as well as, membership in groups focused on personal development.

In support of this suggestion for our readers and followers, we have formed a *Facebook Community* to provide a place where like-minded people can share strategies and wins, exchange and explore ideas, ask questions, provide encouragement and even some accountability. You can join this community by going to: Join Us on Facebook) https://www.facebook.com/groups/CreateTheChange/).

Noticed we used the word community. You might recall that community can be a key factor in helping replace old habits and form new ones. When people with a common motivation work together, it becomes a powerful change tool for all the members. This online community essentially becomes a mastermind group. Take a minute now to join the group, share your thoughts and tell us about the change you'd like to create.

And finally, let us leave you with this one exercise. It's simple and powerful:

While there may be several items or areas in which you wish to bring change in your life, we want you to choose the one you feel is the most important. Now, allocate a minimum of thirty minutes of your schedule each day to think and work on creating this particular change you want to see. Your goal is to make this time with yourself a habit.

Enter it on your digital calendar for the same time each day and treat it as you would a doctor's appointment. You might even set a recurring alarm on your mobile phone. These become the cue for your new habit loop.

Next, is the routine for this new habit. This will be the actual activity or work during this period that moves you closer to achieving your goal. It is important that you have previously mapped out what you need to do to hit your target.

The last five minutes of your designated time should be used for visualizing yourself having achieved the objective. Be sure to engage as many of your senses as possible in the visualization process. (Revisit the section on visualization earlier in the book).

How will you feel when you achieve it? Mentally experience the end result. By doing this, you are mentally conditioning your subconscious mind and it will begin attracting to you the internal and external resources necessary to achieve the goal.

Finally, determine a reward that you can give yourself for the completion of the routine. Be sure it is something you really value so it is a strong incentive.

As it becomes stronger, we encourage you to add additional wants and desires to this habit process.

We are going to remind you, once again. Action is the final key to creating what you want to see in your life. For that reason, this essential habit will serve you well, keeping you focused and consistently in action toward your goal.

Through this book, we've given you the power to bring great change in your life. If you've derived benefit from reading this, we want to challenge you to do one more thing. Help others to accomplish the same by passing this power on. Send a copy of this book to family, friends or co-worker.

NOW, GO OUT AND CREATE THE CHANGE
YOU WANT TO SEE IN YOUR LIFE!

Note: One of our goals is to find different ways to use this book to change lives. Every three minutes a child is born with a cleft lip and palate. This is a tremendous emotional and psychological burden for these children and their families. In order to help make a major change in the lives of these children, a portion of the proceeds from the sale of this book will go to Smile Train. Smile Train's medical partners provide 100%-free surgeries and comprehensive cleft care to children around the world. Visit their Smile Train website (www.smiletrain.org/).

ABOUT THE AUTHORS

Arthur "Ski" Swiatkowski is a speaker, author, consultant and coach, who has been studying and working in the areas of personal development, leadership and performance improvement for the past 40 years. Using as a foundation, the works of great minds like Wayne Dyer, Tony Robbins, Dr. Norman Vincent Peale, Stephen Covey and many others, he has developed a special approach to the many facets of business and personal life. This approach focuses on living consciously, plus the power of the human mind to initiate change and the ability to create an abundant life from that power.

His many years in management and corporate leadership provided him with a laboratory with which to test the practicality of various theories and trends in performance improvement and people development. He has trained thousands of people in the financial services industry and spoken at conferences all across the country.

With an active background in sports, which included playing collegiate football, semi-professional football and men's lacrosse, he leveraged these experiences to gain additional insights into our ability to develop physically, mentally, emotionally and spiritually in order to thrive in our competitive world.

A graduate of Drexel University, he lives in Bucks County, PA. Ski is married to Sharon (his wife of 45 years), a retired RN, turned handy-woman, who has done everything around their house except write this book. They've raised two wonderful children, Alexandra and Seth, and have gained a lovely daughter-in-law, Sonya. They all continue to inspire him. To learn more about Ski's work, visit www.RadicalPerformance.net.

Jim Donovan, a native New Yorker, has implemented the timeless principles in his books to first, turn his own life around, and then to devote his life to helping others do the same for more than 25 years. Jim practices these principles every day and is living proof that they work.

A bestselling author, whose books are published in 26 countries, and a motivational speaker, he has touched the lives of literally hundreds of thousands of people who desire a better life.

Crossing all ethnic, age, and gender barriers, his simple message has been embraced by teenagers and seniors alike. From business leaders to single parents, people throughout the world are improving the quality of their lives by following the simple techniques in his books and programs. To learn more about Jim's work, visit www.JimDonovan.com.

SOURCES, CREDITS AND ACKNOWLEDGEMENTS

ACKNOWLEDGEMENTS

Vince Papale's Speaker page
(www.vincepapale.com/bookvince.html)

Brian Propp's web page
(www.brianpropp.com)

Brian Propp's photo credit: *Bill McCay at Tournament Shooters* (www.tournamentshooters.com-).

CHARITABLE ORGANIZATIONS

These organizations will receive a portion of the profits of this book are:

OPERATION SMILE

Operation Smile (https://www.operationsmile.org/)
Our Mission

We estimate that there are 5 million children waiting for care in the 34 countries where we work.

The majority of these children are unable to receive the medical care they need because it is too costly, far away, or specialized. Because of this, being born with a cleft condition can be fatal. If a child survives, they may face bullying and social isolation.

Through our expertise in treating cleft lip and cleft palate, we create solutions that deliver safe surgery to people where it's needed most.

PHILADOPTABLES

Philadoptables (https://philadoptables.org/)
Mission Statement

Philadoptables' mission is to assist those who assist Philly's most at-risk animals: rescue organizations, individuals and animals shelters, especially ACCT Philly, the City's open-intake shelter.

Our wholly volunteer-run organization does this by

1.   Helping animal rescue organizations that save Philly's homeless animals by providing financial assistance for medical or other needs.
2.   Funding ACCT Philly shelter improvements, equipment and other needs.

3. Communicating ACCT Philly's needs, including the need for funding, volunteers, and fosters; and promoting ACCT Philly's animals for adoption, foster and rescue.
4. Helping pet owners with basic care for their pets so they are not forced to surrender their pets to ACCT Philly.
5. Helping community cats stay well and safe in their communities.

RESEARCH CREDITS

Content reference on the theory of multiple intelligences based on research of psychologist, Dr. Howard Gardner

A content reference for chapter on decisions came from the book:

"Thinking, Fast and Slow" by psychologist Daniel Kahneman, Farrar, Straus and Giroux; (April 2, 2013)

A content resource for the chapter on habits was:

"The Power of Habit" by Charles Duhigg, Random House Trade Paperbacks (January 7, 2014)

RESOURCES

Links to EFT sites for more info

Gary Craig, (https://www.emofree.com), the originator of EFT tapping offers training in EFT for Professionals and serious students, lists of Practitioners and more.

EFT Universe (https://www.eftuniverse.com), Developed by author Dawson Church, EFT Universe contains hundreds of video's, trainings,

Veterans Stress Project (www.stressproject.org),

Cover design, Jim Eagle
www.James Eagle.com